NEW WRITING / BOOK TALK / NEWS AND REVIEWS

THE READER

D0766126

No. 40 WINTER 2010

Published by The Reader Organisation at The University of Liverpool.
Supported by:

the reader
organisation

UNIVERSITY OF
LIVERPOOL

EDITOR   Philip Davis

DEPUTY EDITOR   Sarah Coley
CO-EDITORS   Maura Kennedy
                                    Angela Macmillan
                                    Eleanor McCann
                                    Brian Nellist
                                    John Scrivener

NEW YORK EDITOR   Enid Stubin

ADDRESS   The Reader Magazine
                                    The Reader Organisation
                                    19 Abercromby Square
                                    Liverpool L69 7ZG

EMAIL   magazine@thereader.org.uk
WEBSITE   www.thereader.org.uk
BLOG   www.thereaderonline.co.uk

DISTRIBUTION   See p. 128
SUBSCRIPTION INFORMATION   See p.78

ISBN 978-0-9558733-9-3

SUBMISSIONS

The Reader genuinely welcomes submissions of poetry, fiction, essays, readings and thought. We publish professional writers and absolute beginners. Send your manuscript with SAE please to:

The Reader Office, 19 Abercromby Square, Liverpool L69 7ZG, UK.

Printed and bound in the European Union by Bell and Bain Ltd, Glasgow

THE READER ORGANISATION

NEWS AND EVENTS

CHRISTMAS GIFTS

Looking for the perfect gift for someone who loves books and reading, or someone that would love to be read to? We can offer something for everyone, reader or non-reader, so that the delights of reading can be shared and enjoyed at any time:

A Little, Aloud
RRP £9.99 ISBN 9780701185633
The perfect Christmas gift for friends and family. This anthology of poetry and prose has been compiled and edited by Angela Macmillan and comes from her experiences of reading in Get Into Reading groups. Stories and poetry to delight everyone; from Shakespeare to Seamus Heaney, Black Beauty to Madame Bovary. **See page 72 for details of great offer for Reader magazine readers!**

Free Magazine Gift Subscriptions
Give the gift of reading, not once, but four times a year. Renew your subscription to The Reader in time for Christmas and get a gift subscription absolutely free! See p. 78 for details.

PENNY READINGS
6.30pm, 5th December, St George's Hall, Liverpool

Our hugely popular festive celebration of all things Dickensian is just around the corner! Come along for reading, singing, and the all important reader rafle… you'll be put in the best of spirits for Christmas time.

For the first time ever, there will be an event on the same day for the children and young people of Merseyside: **The Ha'penny Readings!** This will be held at 2.30pm at St George's Hall, where there will be singing, dancing, presents for those who attend and, of course, some magical readings.

Tickets for both events are available from 22nd November at Waterstone's Bold Street (Liverpool) and Birkenhead Central Library. Be quick!

KEEP UP TO DATE!

Visit our blog to keep in touch with all Reader Organisation matters:

www.thereaderonline.co.uk

CONTENTS

JOANNA TROLLOPE

READING FROM
SAKI, THE LUMBER ROOM
AT THE LAUNCH OF

A LITTLE, ALOUD

SEE p. 72 FOR GREAT OFFER
FOR READERS

EDITORIAL

THE BIG 40

Philip Davis

Mr Albert lived next-door-but-one to us in the early sixties, with his wife and young son. They shared a drive with our immediate neighbours, the Johnsons, who were the most buttoned-up English couple you can imagine (he collected stamps, she migraines). Mr Albert, who must have just turned forty back then, was himself old-fashioned. He would lift his trilby hat to my mother by several inches whenever we met him, to show a pale bald head with one plait of black hair draped across it, and then remove his pipe for brief and stilted conversation. He was said to have been a school-teacher but had suffered a nervous breakdown and was now a local government clerk. My mother approved his politeness and sense of quiet privacy, but thought his wife was sharp with him.

It was a surprise when Mr Albert rang the doorbell violently one evening. We were not a family much in favour of the doorbell, save as an early warning device. Howard Jacobson is this year's Booker prize-winner, bless him, and you may remember he wrote for us back in issue 31: a *Reader*-Booker even sounds like a Jewish formula for turning a curse into a congratulation. At any rate, in one of his early novels he describes how Jewish families of his own childhood were still mindful of the midnight knock on the door, at any time of the day. Hooder-hell-izzat was anxiety's cry. Not to answer was normal. To hide under the bed was apparently the Jacobson family's more extreme version.

Mr Albert had been running noisily from one house to another around our little cul-de-sac, no hat, no pipe, no jacket or tie. He had knocked first of all, again and again, at the house of the Johnsons but they would not admit him. Nobody would. I was scared: we could hear him and see him from the window, running from door to door, when he rang at ours. And frankly, I was on the side of the Johnsons for the first time in my young life. But my parents were not. Packing me upstairs, they opened our door and let him in. An ambulance was coming for him, he said, to take him away. They sat him down in our living room and gave him, from that bottle that lasted us from one Christmas to the year after next, a glass of sherry. He stayed about half an hour till the ambulance came, when there was a quieter ring at the bell, and he walked away quietly with the men.

'Why did you let him in?' I asked my dad soon after. 'Nobody did,' was the shrugged answer, 'Somebody should. The man's dignity.' At that moment I immediately and whole-heartedly despised those Johnsons. My father resigned from the Conservative party around this time, a volunteer local party-worker, in opposition to their new strict immigration policy. They told him he should stay on and fight the policy from within, which he knew was utterly disingenuous and quite hopeless. Not a man for poetry he knew somewhere in his heart the lines written at the base of the Statue of Liberty:

> **Give me your tired, your poor,**
> **Your huddled masses yearning to breathe free,**
> **The wretched refuse of your teeming shore,**
> **Send these, the homeless, tempest-tost to me,**
> **I lift my lamp beside the golden door!**

But we never saw Mr Albert again at our door. There was, I now remember, a boy, Clive Turney, when I first went to school. We didn't make much of him. He was hardly there and when he was, he was very pale and very quiet. Then one day he wasn't, his place was empty, and soon after there was a poster in the classroom about a charity for leukaemia. My mother explained the connection.

I first met Howard Jacobson in 1976. I had been invited down to Cornwall, to the family holiday-home, by my Cambridge Ph.D supervisor Wil Sanders, now much missed. He and Howard were writing a book together, *Shakespeare's Magnanimity*, eventually published in 1978. But Howard was no longer in academe; he was running some sort of arty-crafty shop – there were a million such – in Boscastle. He came over to Wil's place one evening and for no good reason except perhaps that he demanded it, the three of us played Monopoly together – the famous property board-game. Playing Monopoly with Jacobson was like being trapped in a field of Egyptian wheat before an Old Testament combine harvester. I never found out what happened. Hotels went up everywhere in a whirr of Jacobsonian business; inexplicable rents were demanded with intolerable menaces; what was usually a three-hour bore was over in thirty minutes. Wil looked on amiably, a helpless bankrupt, quoting poor Orlando, the younger brother in *As You Like It*: 'Only in the world I fill up a place which may be better supplied when I have made it empty.' I have never played Monopoly since that trauma.

But I think of all these things together as we come towards Christmas when at The Reader Organisation's Dickens Penny Readings in St George's Hall, we shall read aloud again as we always do from *A Christmas Carol*. Especially that place, after a penitent Scrooge has seen the poor boy in the street, sent him off to buy a turkey as big as himself for the Cratchits, and now goes knocking at his nephew's house to try to take up the old, much rejected offer of a place at the Christmas table:

'Why bless my soul!' cried Fred, 'who's that?'
'It's I. Your uncle Scrooge. I have come to dinner. Will you let me in, Fred?'

And then Dickens, who makes us laugh and makes us cry, does that other thing of his for a split second in making us wait. Not every contrition is in time; not every offer is continually open, just because one's changed. Will you, Fred? Then the release:

Let him in! It is a mercy he didn't shake his arm off.

The Reader is 40 with this issue. We are not, I hope, maturely middle-aged. If anything, we are angrier and warmer, and we'll shake your arm off. Do we want to be a pure poetry magazine? NO! Do we want to be an academic journal? NO! Do we want to be a version of the Sunday book reviews? For God's sake, NO! Do we want to offer you easy reads or, if not that, then intellectual abstractions? NO and again NO! We hold a place in the world, however little, which otherwise, we fear, would be empty or, rather, non-existent. A place between and across all these things: poetry, fiction, essay, social mission, real thinking, unashamed emotion, belief in books. If nobody does, somebody should. We do.

Editor's Picks
Our longest short story ever is actually an adaptation of a chapter from a novel in progress by **Tessa Hadley**. True to our desire to move across all forms, we also have her writing an essay on one of our neglected favourites, the novelist and short-story writer **Elizabeth Taylor**. The film-maker **Terence Davies** gives us his Liverpool memories, while the poetry of **Blake Morrison**, **Peter Robinson**, **Emma McGordon** and **Richard Meier** remembers life's great changes. Add to the mix the theologian **Catherine Pickstock** on Hopkins, and **Michael Schmidt**, poet, critic and editor of *PN Review*, on Kipling. And don't forget to buy *A Little, Aloud* for your friends and family at Christmas. Do you hear?

FACE TO FACE

MEET THE POET

BLAKE MORRISON on p.13

Should your poems be read silently or aloud?

I'd like my poems to be read on the page, with silent, monk-like concentration, but also out loud, in the pub (or theatre or festival tent or round a table). Poetry becomes richer the more it is re-read – it doesn't exhaust its meaning or expend all its energy first time round. But for a poem to resonate it has to make an initial impact and that's where sound is so crucial – to say the words aloud, rolling them in your mouth and testing them on the air, is vital not just to the composition of a poem but to its reception.

Which poet would you like to have met?

Auden, as I once a had very weird experience where I was convinced that the poem 'Nightmail' began 'North, North, North to the country of the Clyde and the Firth of Forth.' I even read out the words from a book to my friend. It was only when looking for the line break for an essay I was writing that I realised these lines do not exist. I have searched every copy of the poem I can find. I need to ask Auden if there is a version that starts like that. It's a mild obsession.

EMMA McGORDON on p.34

RICHARD MEIER on pp.45 & 49

Has a poem ever changed your mind?

Before I read Les Murray's 'The Quality of Sprawl' I'd have thought it impossible to write a poem about this subject matter in this kind of way. I'd have been fairly adamant (and therefore lacking in sprawl I imagine) that you could not espouse a 'loose-limbed' philosophy to life using a loose-limbed/free-verse approach – that you'd end up with a slack mess of a poem. But this exhilarating, chutzpah-packed performance is an ideal match of form and content, and a great antidote to any fixed ideas about form being the be-all-and-end-all or that less is always more.

Which poet would you like to have met?

It's a toss-up between the Elizabethan poet Michael Drayton, who was from Polesworth, close to where I live, and whose long poem 'Poly-olbion' I'm more than a little obsessed by, and RS Thomas, whose books I go back to all the time. In the end I'd probably have to come down on the side of the great Welshman. By all accounts he could be hard work, but if all else failed we could always talk about birds – he was a fellow birdwatcher.

MATT MERRITT on p.59

Should your poems be read silently or aloud?

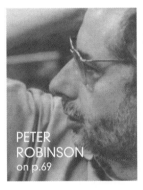

PETER ROBINSON on p.69

My poems are written with the idea that they will be best experienced when read out loud, but that they can be appreciated silently if the silent reading involves an imaginative embodiment of the poem's formal dynamic in the reader. The shape of the poem — its rhythm, pitch, tone, rhyme and all the minutiae of cadence, enjamb-ment, caesura, and so forth — are to provide the reader not only with intellectual and emotional stimulation, but also an experience of physical integrity and well-being. That's how they aim to transform difficulties into benefits.

Should your poems be read silently or aloud?

I like all poems to be read out loud, mine and other people's. I go to as many readings as I can to hear how the poet handles their own material, and websites such as The Poetry Archive that host video recordings of readings are a blessing.

When I write, I speak every word of every line so I can hear the rhythm and evocation of the words. The voice is so important to me because I am very dyslexic and a very poor reader. When I encounter a new poet on the page, I often struggle to get the feel of their text. But when I hear that poet read, their work comes to life.

LINDA CHASE on p.88

BLAKE MORRISON

POETRY

BLAKE MORRISON

Carissimo

Remember the year the sandbank appeared?
We swam out through breakers for fifty yards
then fetched up on a magic yellow colony
and marched about as if we owned the place,
two giants on an unmapped island,
the tiny waves like excited natives
clamouring around our feet.

On the way back a tethered speedboat was rocking.
We slithered up the side of it and in,
and lay among ropes and life-jackets,
the sun on my back as I tasted salt,
and you whispering something,
the same few syllables over and over,
like water swishing in the hull.

At the time it sounded like 'trespassers'.

The dressing gown

Twenty years on, your dressing gown
hangs from the bedroom door
waiting to come back in style.

Short, thin, with mauve and blue stripes,
it was more for the beach
than round the house,

a thing you'd drop in a heap
as you ran into the sea
then towel yourself dry with afterwards,

stretching the collar tight like a loofah
to rub that itch you couldn't get at
in the middle of your back.

I took it with your other things:
the shoes, shirts, blazer with brass buttons,
all since discarded, unworn.

For months it smelled of talc
or engine oil or maybe the sea -
of you anyway.

Now it's mustier, the colours fading,
the posture too slack for you
('keep those shoulders straight!'),

nothing in the pockets but fluff.
I should take it to the dump
but first I try it on,

feeling it settle round me
like skin I've slipped inside,
and when I look

there's you in the mirror,
serious, head tilted, sizing things up:
'A perfect fit.'

FICTION

BUTTONS

Tessa Hadley

I was staying over at my Nana's. I was ten. I woke miraculously early, which was unusual for me – as a rule my transition out of the rich silt of my dreams was sluggish and reluctant, even in those child-hood days. The blankets at Nana's were meagre, ex-army, in prickly grey wool with an oily smell. They would only stay tucked in down both sides if you kept unnaturally still, which I never could – in my sleep I had shifted and burrowed, the blankets had come untucked, and a little slit of freezing air was probing along my warm body like a knife. Then I rolled over onto the inflexible hand of my plastic teenage doll. Ordinarily, I would have thrown out the doll (I wasn't a callous parent, only brusque sometimes), wrapped my feet in my nightie and my arms round my knees, doused my sight in the snug me-smelling nest, set off determinedly to find my dreams again. Sometimes if I woke up I turned the bedding around and put the pillow at the foot, and to Nana's dismay went back to sleep upside down – which was a revelation of a different room, another world-order. But the doll's hand that morning seemed to poke me with a message: 'Arise!' (I was reading a lot of books set in the past, which was grander and better.)

It was Saturday. It was spring – yellow squares of light commanded me, from where they were transforming the unlined curtains at the

TESSA HADLEY

window, making weightless the heavy bars of purple wound with a clinging vine. Light even seemed to be ballooning the curtains, swelling them out into the room – I had forgotten that I'd dragged the window up before I went to sleep (Nana believed in fresh air, but only an inch of it – I liked to stick my head out to look at the dark). It must have been remarkably early, because I couldn't hear a sound in the house; almost always by the time I came to consciousness Nana was already busy with her housework – sweeping and wiping and soaking, smooth-ing out brown paper bags and saving them, un-knotting scraps of string and winding them into balls. I was the first to break the skin of the day, stepping out of the blankets into it, the lino striking its frozen cold up through the warm soles of my feet.

When I parted the curtains and looked out, I saw what I'd never seen – that for hours before humans were up the cats had sole posses-sion of the gardens, just when these were most gleaming and renewed by their dip in night. Cats were dotted around the vantage points like sentinels. All the familiar scrappy back landscape – trellis and dustbins and old bikes and crazy paving stepping stones – was glazed in light, and had a surprising sealed and secretive power in its owners' absence, holding something back, revealed as meaning more than just its use-fulness. Glass windows black with dirt were a shed's eye pits. Nana's lilies-of-the-valley set out on a forced march down the cracks between the pavings. A neighbour's tabby, Timmy, glanced disdainfully up at me, interrupted in triumphing over his enemies from a wall-top; he came purring and butting my hand in the evenings when I gave him milk, but didn't deign to know me in this moment of his vigilance.

If I got dressed, I thought, I could go out into this – what could stop me? Because no one had ever thought of it, I'd never even been forbid-den to go out before anyone was up. My latchkeys were warm on their ribbon against my chest, under my vest – I wasn't supposed to sleep in them in case I strangled myself, but I always did, because I couldn't bear the anticipation, dropping them down my front in the morning, braced to recoil from their ice-blow. I could go home by myself, without telling Nana, and surprise my mother. Gleefully I imagined the reversal of our roles: Mum's tousled head raised, blinking and sleepy and astonished, from the pillow at the end of her sofa pulled into its night-position; my own bright wakefulness, airy and full of implications from its journey through the outdoors. For once, I would have the advantage of her.

Pulling on my knickers and socks and slacks, buttoning my ruched check shirt, diving into the V-neck of the jumper Nana had knitted in rust-brown stocking stitch, I was light-headed with sensations of freedom and power I had no name for yet. All the time I was listening out for Nana. Now I had started, I couldn't bear to be prevented. I had worried sometimes about how I would make the transition into being grown-up – how did you know when to begin? Now I understood that you stepped out into it, as simply as into a day.

*

People forget that in 1966 there were still bombsites. It took a long time to stitch back together that fabric of our cities ripped cruelly open by the war. (Or rather, not to stitch it back at all, but tear the fabric out and throw it away and put something different and uglier in its place.) Every time I made my way home from Nana's I had to walk past an open area where bombs had fallen: you could still make out different wallpapers on the high standing walls, distinguishing the squares of vanished rooms, washed by the rain to faint ghosts of their former patterns; traces of a staircase in a zig-zag pattern climbing up; doors opening onto nothing. Whatever desolation there must have been at first was softened and naturalised after two decades; with their grassy uneven footing, heaps of stones overgrown with buddleia and fireweed, the sites were as consoling as gardens. When I had friends to stay we played out there; boys rode their bikes round on the grass in the evenings. Our flat was on the first floor of a spindly Georgian terrace in Kingsdown, Bristol; it was on a high bluff, and from our back windows we surveyed the plain of Broadmead sprawling below, punctuated then by the spires of churches, ruined and otherwise, only just beginning to be drowned under a tide of office blocks and shopping centres, a new world.

In my mind's eye now, our street as it was then is as raddled as the ancient buildings in early photographs of London slums (I was looking at them the other day in the V and A): black and white, teetering, neglected, somehow manifesting on their exterior – as intricately as embroidery – the layers upon layers of complex and crowded arrangements for living inside, the revolution of generations inside the same space circumscribed by wood or brick or stone. There was broken glass in some of the windows in our street; at others filthy torn lace curtains, or bedspreads hooked up to keep out the light. A frightening old woman next door wore a long black dress like a Victorian. Our house was five stories tall if you counted the basement, which was on garden level at the back; Mrs. Watts – kindly but with a goitrous bulge on her neck I couldn't bear to look at – lived in there with her elderly son. (She used to say, 'Can you believe it, he was my little boy?') And beneath the basement was a windowless cellar – I had been down there, Mrs. Watts had let me. Its mineral cold was dense as water, and there were stalactites growing from the vaulted ceiling; I knew what they were because we'd been on a school trip to Wookey Hole caves. They used to say there were iron rings in some of the Bristol cellars, where they chained the slaves – and secret tunnels leading to the docks. In Bristol stories there were always slaves and sugar and tobacco.

A staircase wound around the deep stairwell at the house's core: the handrail was polished wood and the banister rods were shaky in their sockets, some of them missing (I had bad dreams in which they gave way and I fell down towards the bottom). There were two rooms on each floor, and for the whole house one bathroom, two toilets. Brass brackets for gas lamps on the wall had never been taken out; the sash cords in the long windows were all broken, and we had to prop them open with pieces of batten. Sometimes I'm nostalgic now for that intricate decay, as if it was a vanished subtler style, overlaid by the banality of making over and smartening up that came later. My mother never was nostalgic. She was apologetic, if ever anyone came to see us, that we had to live anywhere so seedy – either apologetic, depending on who the visitor was, or steely in her prideful refusal to acknowledge anything wrong. She got out, the minute she had the chance.

You should see our old road these days. I shouldn't think those houses change hands for much less than a million. Everyone now covets the 'original features', the spindly height, the long walled gardens, the view. Those places sing with money and improvement. Nana's little Victorian box around the corner, which we used to think was so much 'better', can't compare.

*

Once I'd pulled Nana's front door gradually and quietly shut behind me, I couldn't get back inside unless I rang the bell – I'd never needed a key for Nana's because she was always in. The day was less resplendent already, pulling a veil of grey across the glory it had shown me. From somewhere far off came the ruminative stop-start of the milkman's electric float, but still I had the morning more or less to myself: I could hear the crepe-soled creak of my sandals on the pavement, the jangled clang of the gate as it closed with finality after me, as if these sounds were bouncing off the silent houses opposite – I could almost see my surprising self, setting out about my own business in the streets. My hair in those days was chopped off in a clean line at shoulder length, fawn-coloured and uninteresting. I had my windcheater zipped up and my hands in its pockets; I fancied I walked with a rather masculine casual bravado. I wasn't interested at that point of my life in being girlish – what I admired were horses, and the boyish-girls who hung around horses. I thought that girls who cared about clothes and pop stars had fallen for a humiliating trick, which I viewed with a mixture of contempt and envy. At school camp the boys had come into the girls' tents after lights out and queued up humbly to kiss a certain girl, Helen Warren, an acknowledged beauty. In the coach on the way home from camp the girls had sung 'We've got the best boy-friend in the world...' I accepted with a child's fatalism that I was shut out from an inner circle of excitement, and was at least half relieved.

Turning the corner at the end of Nana's street, I started along a path which was a shortcut across the bombsite. When I saw a man sitting facing away from me on one of the broken low walls, it was too late to go back, but my heart beat with shy anxiety: I hated the idea of any strange adult speaking to me, I was always afraid they would roar something I would fail to understand, resent some trespass I couldn't know I had committed. Wearing a dark overcoat, the man was sitting bent over, his head in his hands. Because it was so early, the morning seemed to wrap us up alone together; I longed for him not to bring down my mood of exalted independence. The path ran close behind where he sat; hurrying past, I could make out the black cloth of his coat, worn to gingery brown across the shoulders, freckled with scurf from his hair. I thought it was strange that an adult man came out to sit alone on a pile of stones: I couldn't imagine either of my uncles doing it. I didn't know much about men, but in my experience they were always purposefully on their way somewhere.

Then I realised it was Mrs. Watts' son Clive. Perhaps I hadn't rec-ognised him because it was the first time I'd ever seen him anywhere beyond the end of our street. He lifted his head out of his hands and peered over his shoulder at me: doleful long face, unshaven cheeks and chin, the beard-growth specked with silver. The inner rim of his lower eyelids was lined in sore, wet red.

– Come and look at this, he said.

Clive was strange. He had had meningitis when he was three and his twin sister had died of it. We had lived in the same house since I could remember, but he and I had an unspoken agreement not to ac-knowledge one another, except when our intercourse was mediated by our mothers. – Can you believe he had yellow curls once? Mrs Watts would say, pushing her fingers through his hair so that he ducked. – Say hello to Stella, Clive.

– Say hello to Clive, my mother would order, shoving me sharply in the small of the back. She was full of ostentatious pity for the 'poor thing', but also thought it might be better for everyone if he was 'put away', whatever that meant. – It's not much of a life, she said, as if she knew.

I'm not sure whether Clive really recognised me that morning. We never spoke about it afterwards. I might have just been any passing little girl. I didn't want to go over to him but it didn't occur to me to disobey:

there was something commanding in the way he spoke without pream-ble or the fake joviality adults sometimes put on. Warily I stepped over the wall into the ghost-interior of the vanished house. Swallows were flitting and shrieking inside the space, they nested there.

– Look what I've found, Clive said.

There was a disordered heap on the ground between where his two brown boots were planted; one of these boots was made up with a special thick sole, because of his sloping, dragging walk.

– What is it?

– Buttons.

– What d'you mean, buttons?

– Come and look.

I saw that he was right: thrown against the wall, fallen into the cracks in the stones and rolled into the grass there was a improbable slew of buttons of all sorts – thousands of them, much more than a handful or even a tin full. I crouched down to them, wondering, not touching yet. – Who do they belong to? How did they get here?

– They must have belonged to the woman who lived in this house.

I said they couldn't have – I played here often, and I'd never seen the buttons before. Someone must have come and dumped them. Clive ignored my reasoning. He said he had known the woman who once lived here, and they must be hers; I began to believe him because he was so certain. Did he mean a woman who had lived here before the bomb fell? Some of these buttons were old: carved jet ones, brass ones with military insignia. But others looked modern: coloured plastic ones, like the ones my Nana put on my cardigans, were still sewn onto the cards they'd been bought on. Some were fastened into sets – miniature mother-of-pearl buttons for baby clothes, pink glass drops – but most of the buttons were loose, jumbled chaotically together: a coral rose, wooden toggles, a diamanté buckle, big yellow bone squares, buttons made of bamboo and some that looked like amber; these exotica offset against a background of hundreds or thousands of ordinary black and brown and white ones.

Something about the sheer exaggerated multiplicity of the buttons – the fact you couldn't get to the bottom of them – started an ache of desire in my chest. I thought that Clive was feeling the same thing. He breathed through his mouth noisily, staring down between his boots. His cheeks under their strong beard-growth were dramatic, hollow as if they'd been carved out with something clumsy like an axe; the raw mask of a man's face was overlaid on his life which was more like the life of a child. Every afternoon Clive was allowed to wander out along our road – he always stopped at one particular lamp post, as if it was a limit his mother had set him; he would be standing there when we children came home from school, hunched over, smoking and watching us, wearing his overcoat in winter, a short grey mac in summer. We squealed and ran past him – even I did, pretending I didn't know him. Every tea time, Mrs. Watts came out to bring him back, pulling him coaxingly by the hand. She endured the publicity of this daily comic theatre – small, bent, fat old woman tugging at tall, scowling, resisting man – with a patient, habituated smile, shown around to anyone who might see them.

This morning Clive and I were matched, in having slipped out momentarily from control. I wondered if he came to the bombsite every day, and if Mrs. Watts knew he came. – We could take them home for your mother, I generously suggested, feeling self-sacrificial, responsible.

But I wanted the coral rose for myself, or the buckle.

Shocking me, Clive scuffed some of the buttons into the dirt with his normal boot.

– Don't touch them. Leave them, he scolded, as if he was angry with me.

Close up, I could smell his familiar smell, the same as in their basement flat: closeted and staled, like damp feather cushions or mouldy bread, mixed with something perfumed he put on his hair (or his mother did). I didn't like the stubborn obliviousness with which he blocked me, not taking any notice of my separate existence, though he had called me over in the first place. Reasonably, I pointed out that if anyone wanted them they shouldn't have thrown them away, but he didn't listen, he was preoccupied, sorting through the buttons with clumsy yellow-stained fingers as if he was searching for something, his expression intent. Clear snot glistened on the fluted curves of his upper lip. Crouched on my haunches, balancing on the balls of my feet with my hands on my knees, I watched him jealously.

Really, where could so many buttons have come from? Someone might have had a button shop, and given it up: but then, why pour out the cornucopia here? Whoever it was must have emptied out drawers-full of them, must have carried them first from the road across to this spot. I was frustrated that Clive was not a real adult who could offer answers – though I knew that just as often they only dismissed the questions. 'Oh Stella. Don't be silly. Whatever for?' The buttons were seductive, opening floodgates of fantasy. One outsize one Clive turned up and held to the light was pearly white, so translucent it was almost green, carved with something like a leggy bird with a long beak, perhaps a heron. I had never thought with any interest about clothes before that moment, except dolls' clothes; but I had a heady vision suddenly of this button as the single fastening of a black velvet cape, full-length, dragging behind me along the marble floor of a place I'd never been. – Arise,

I thought again to myself, as I had in bed. – Behold.

I couldn't help reaching out to take it.

Clive smacked at my hand.

– They're not yours, I said indignantly. – They're anybody's.

Then he pushed me hard on the knee, so that I overbalanced and fell backwards. He stood up and towered over me. Behind his looming silhouette I saw the sky, screaming swallows, the ragged top of a wall. It was a surprise to be reminded of how wholly Clive filled out his big man's body. Because of the child's life he led, traipsing everywhere after his mother, it was easy to discount his grown-up shape as if he'd only borrowed it, the same way girls dressed up in their mothers' shoes and lipstick. Looking up at him now, I saw Clive's size fitted as inevitably around him as mine did around me, and that he was at home in it; in fact, because he walked sloppily and mumbled to himself, he was more deeply burrowed away inside his body than other grown-ups were. Other grown-ups, especially women, had learned somehow to live on the surfaces of theirs, controlling them and presenting a prepared version of them to the world.

*

Sometimes when Clive stood under the lamp post and watched the children coming home from school, you could see he was rubbing himself, with his hand down in his trousers – not in any kind of sinful frenzy, more as if he was only half aware of doing it, comforting and reassuring himself. There was an old man who did something like this at the swimming baths too, sitting on the edge of the pool, staring at the girls squealing and splashing, rocking himself in a rolling movement back and forwards against the pool's rim, taking his weight on his hands. If you caught the pool-man's eye he was jeering and slippery; whereas if Clive ever looked at you, he was contemptuous as if you had nothing for him. I knew it comforted men to touch themselves. I had seen Uncle Ray and Uncle Frank putting their hands down there, adjusting themselves inside their underwear, sniffing their fingers afterwards. My mother would make a little face of distaste at it, clicking her tongue. Auntie Jean would dig her elbow in Frank's ribs, reminding him he was in company.

– Don't look, my mother snapped if she saw Clive busy in his trousers, closing her expression tight shut as if it was my fault, for shaming her. – Cross the road! Stella!

I ought to have been afraid of him that morning but I wasn't. I had been relieved, all along, that it was Clive I met on the bombsite and not a stranger, who might have disrupted my possession of the special day; in relation to Clive I was still powerful and not obliterated. When he stood looming over me I felt more outrage than fear, and rolled over, scrambling to my feet, dusting off my knees, which were not grazed but lightly stuck with bits of gravel and grass. I wasn't hurt in the least, only shocked and humiliated.

– You're not supposed to push me!

He took a step towards me, making a threatening gesture with his hand in the air like the one my mother made to me sometimes. On my dignity I stepped backwards, deliberately insouciant. Then I turned and skipped away.

How I used to love that skipping – two bounces on the one foot, then two on the other – which carried you as fast as seven-league boots, buoyant and flinging forwards, rebounding off the ground each time with double strength. What a loss, when one day I wasn't able to fly along like that any longer, ever again. I can't remember what stopped me first. Was it inhibition, because I grew older and reached the point where I wanted to be seen, like the women who presented themselves so tranquilly and with such poise? Or was it because after I had a child, something was unbound inside me, so that if I ever jumped or ran for a bus I felt my organs churning in a horrible disorder? Which came first? Anyway, I'm still in mourning for my skipping self.

Clive came lumbering after me, but I knew he couldn't catch me. The smack of his heavy boots when he reached the pavement was loud as gunshots in the empty street. I stopped and waited for him by the grocer's shop, where the beige sun-blinds, cracked and torn, were still drawn down inside the windows: between the glass and the blinds was stacked a pyramid of tins of peas, their labels faded almost to intelligibility. I had looked at those peas a thousand times.

– Here, grunted Clive when he caught up with me, stopping at a respectful distance, holding out his big greeny-white fist.

I held out my open hand to him.

He gave me the coral rose and the diamanté buckle.

I still have them.

*

Before I turned the corner into our road, I had put the encounter with Clive out of my mind, though not my new treasures, which I kept clenched tight in my hand. The only thought I spent on him was that I would tell my mother I had 'found them'. Standing facing our front door – I had two keys, one for this and one for the subordinate door to our flat inside – I was the most daunted I had been by my adventure. I had used my keys many times before; but then, I had always been expected. Now, in the street bleached and flattened by its unaccustomed emptiness – though the milkman's float was working its way from the other end – I felt myself discounted, as though normality, in which I was absent, was stronger than I was. The grandeur of our door impressed me for the first time: elevated from the street up its flight of worn steps, with an iron boot scraper set into the stone, and an ancient heavy iron knocker (no one needed to use the knocker, because of the cracked row of plastic bell-pushes to one side, where names were written in ink on slips of card). Inside, I hesitated in the hall, breathing its foggy air of oily linoleum and forgotten coats and shoes, freckled with ruby from the coloured glass in the back door, where steps led down into the garden.

In the room beside the front door lived old Tom with a cleft palate who worked for the Salvation Army; in the room behind his, the woman who worked in the fish and chip shop round the corner and smelled of it. I couldn't hear anyone moving about; on tip-toe, I started up the stairs. My mother would be pleased to see me, wouldn't she? I imagined again her sleepy confusion, coming out of her dreams, focussing gradually on the surprising fact of me; I began to wonder if she might be more annoyed than pleased. A vague light sifted down through the dirty skylight set into the roof (which leaked when it rained); I paused outside our door. In the flat above us lived a couple with a baby I knitted bootees for, and in the attic above them was reticent Geoffrey, who fed me on spoonfuls of condensed milk from an opened tin in his cupboard, and painted huge abstracts in cream and brown and black (he left them behind when he flitted without paying his rent). From Geoffrey's casement windows you could climb out into the lead-lined gutter that ran the length of the terrace, eighteen inches deep, with a stone parapet between it and the street so far below. I had sat out there on the parapet more than once, with my back to the street and my feet in the gutter.

Now I fitted my key into the lock.

I don't know why it didn't occur to me that, if I wasn't there, my mother wouldn't sleep on the sofa but in the bed I thought of as mine, in the bedroom: I was startled, as I let myself into the flat – staggering slightly because the key was still on its ribbon round my neck, and this keyhole was rather high up on the door – to see the sofa untouched, pristine in its daytime identity. She couldn't be up already, could she? But there was no sign of her – and we only had those two rooms. Always, if she was up, she was busy. Because she had to work in the office all day, there was plenty to do at home: vacuuming, dusting, rinsing our clothes through in the sink, ironing them – she called it 'rinsing', as though that made it a lighter and smarter job than washing, less like drudgery. She did all her housework in that spirit of briskly efficient dismissal. The sheets and towels she had to take round to Nana, who heated the copper for them.

She couldn't be out. Her handbag was on the table, her bright silk scarf flopped, plumy and exotic, between its handles. Beside the sink were two tea-cups and two glasses, filled with water to soak. I pulled the door shut very quietly behind me, and stood taking in whatever extraordinary thing had happened. I knew I'd found my mother out in something, although I didn't know what – and I felt nakedly exposed, as if it was me who'd been treacherous. Who had been here with her, while I was away? Was it Auntie Jean? The glasses came out for Jean sometimes. I wanted to go stamping around the room, to assert my right to do it, but I kept stony still. Her coat was on its hanger. Her high heels were kicked off beside the sofa; I knew how she eased her feet out of them, grimacing in relief. I could smell her perfume, and the faint stale-biscuit smell of her nylons, which I liked, as if it was a secret weakness I kept safe for her.

She must be asleep in my bedroom, next door.

I ought to run in and wake her up. Or – a vision of adult competence – I ought to fill the kettle and put it on the gas ring, measure out tea in scoopfuls from the caddy, wake her with breakfast (though she didn't like breakfast in bed: 'What a mess, Stella'). I stared into the kitchen-end of our living room (the kitchenette, she determinedly called it), as if I watched myself progressing through these morning rituals – but without moving from my spot. I was waiting for a sign. I felt the effect of my presence rolling out from me like waves, filling the flat, even though Mum couldn't have heard me come in – she couldn't be awake or she would have called out to me, or appeared at the bedroom door, tying her dressing gown. The noise I had made, unlocking and stumbling in on the end of my ribbon, was only small, but I imagined it as part of that intricate sound-machinery of a house, whose tiny triggers work through the inmates' sleep belatedly, bearing messages. Waves of my being there swelled towards that door and pressed on through it; behind it, even before I heard a sound, I knew something roused and responded.

There was someone in there with her.

The bed – my bed – creaked and sighed in its intimately-known voice under more weight than hers. Someone stirred, rolled over, made free with the pillows – the style was alien in our home, uninhibited and loose and large. Then a growling, deep-throated rumble, one of those satisfied private noises from the borders of sleep, was unmistakeably a man's. I was appalled, invaded. I might have thought he'd murdered my mother and taken her place, if I hadn't heard afterwards her own neat little squeak, dozily humorous and protesting. They were drifting into wakefulness. But what life did my mother share with an unknown man? I had thought I knew everything about her that I needed to.

Who knew her this well, apart from me – to share her sleep with her?

I had never thought of bed before as anything but an innocent place; all of a sudden, I understood differently. Through involuntary association – putting two and two together, making everything – there came into my head a song from the school playground, full of forbidden news, part tail-end of folksong, part dirty joke. 'The first time she met him, she met him in black – all in black, all in black, he laid her on her back...' And so on, through the various colours ('all in green, all in green, he filled her up with cream'), until the twins were due, and born, and dead. Whatever was going on now in my own bedroom, it was garish, violent, unsavoury. My mother was the same as the girls at school camp, kissing in the tent, scorching me and leaving me behind. Their excitement seemed to me then the opposite force to the force of the past, which was in books, and pure.

In a daze of rage I stepped over to the table, felt in Mum's handbag for her purse, slipped the worn clasp, and helped myself to her change – not all of it, two half crowns and a sixpence and a few pennies and halfpence. I had never done such a thing before, or even dreamed of it. I couldn't remember why my right hand was clenched awkwardly shut – when I unlocked my fingers, my palm was grooved with the impress of the sharp edges of the buckle. I put back Mum's purse, tipped the coral button and the buckle onto the table and left them there. Disgust lent me a kind of genius of deftness, so that I exited as soundlessly as if I'd never been inside the room.

*

My hands tasted of hot copper from the pennies. I knew where to wait, because I caught this bus with Mum every Saturday afternoon, to go to the stables where I had my riding lesson. Only the number 83 called at this stop, five minutes walk along the road from our house. Probably a bus would never come, I thought – perhaps they didn't even run in the mornings. How would I know? The stop was outside the high brick wall, topped with broken glass stuck into cement, of a factory which made brake linings (I pictured these as brilliant-coloured, silky); the bus company's yellow tin sign on its concrete post seemed for a long while a forlorn flag announcing nothing, and I felt myself conspicuous and jeered at, though no one passed except the milkman, his bottles chiming.

But an 83 did come. I paid the conductor and he didn't question me, dropping the money in his leather bag and winding my ticket from the machine across his shoulder. I had to change in the city centre, to go to Keynsham; for a long time this second bus sat without a driver while I waited inside, the only passenger, too agonised with shyness to get out and ask whether we were ever leaving. I was hungry also by this time for my breakfast. Eventually we began our slow progress through the suburbs, to the outskirts of the city. Everything I saw from my window at the front, at the top, where my mother never wanted to sit – the rising weekend tide of people in the streets, boys setting out a cricket game on a recreation ground, the bombed-out shell of a church with the grass neatly mown around it, car showrooms with plate glass windows – looked more real, dense with itself, because I saw it alone, not filtered through her. When I stepped down at last at my destination from the platform of the bus, I snuffed up the perfumes of manure and of clogged, rotten ditches overgrown with brambles, rejoicing at the crunch under my sandals of dried mud, grown with sparse grass, set in its deep ruts and tyre tracks, whose forms I broke as I trod. Mud was exhilarating, after the city pavements.

What I think now is that it was such a long way for my mother to bring me on the bus, every Saturday, just for me to have the riding lessons I yearned and pleaded for. No doubt there was an element of snobbery and aspiration in her determination to get me to the lessons, and to pay for them – just as there was in her wanting me to go to grammar school. (We fought to the death about these aspirations, later.) For all I know she was imagining Elizabeth Taylor and National Velvet. But it was still a long way, to Keynsham and back, on her only free day of the week (on Sundays we had to go for dinner to one of my uncles' houses, or to Nana's). She had to get all her shopping done on Saturday mornings. What did she do while I lumbered around the paddock on the backs of the fat little ponies, Dozey and Boy and Melba and Star and Chutney? I think she brought her library book with her (Erle Stanley Gardner or Georgette Heyer or Harold Robbins). I think she boiled the stable girls' electric kettle and made herself instant coffee, and that in fine weather she sat reading and smoking on one of those folding wooden chairs on the collapsing verandah that ran along the end of the pavilion (as we grandly called it – it was really more like an overgrown garden shed). Mostly it wasn't fine weather, and she must have stayed inside where it stank of leather tack and pony nuts, and where in winter they lit a fumy paraffin heater. She took no interest in the horses, and wouldn't go near them.

She waited after the lesson when I was allowed to groom Star, going at him with the body brush, lifting his mane to work underneath, releasing that potent musk smell of his sweat, dusty and greasy. Kissing his nose I made contact, through the hot pelt grown close like stubbly chenille on the hard bone of his skull, with that urgent wordless horse life which moved me so inexpressibly. And then we set out home again, on the two buses.

*

The stables were at the back of a grand old abandoned house where nobody lived; the couple who ran them had a ramshackle bungalow in the grounds. Jilly was fierce, lean and sun-dried; Budge (their surname was Budgen) tubby and uneasily jovial. They were both perpetually distracted in an aura of money-anxiety and failure; even though the place must have run itself, pretty much. They had to buy the feed and equipment, but most of the work was done for free by a clique of girls fanatical for horses. The great prize was to be allowed to ride the ponies down bareback to the field, after the lessons were over. These girls were older than I was, thirteen or fourteen, and I was in awe of their swagger and their loud talk about feed supplements and gymkhanas (a lot of this was wishful thinking – we didn't go to many gymkhanas). Their ringleader was Karen, decisive and devoid of humour, with a stubby neat figure, startling light blue eyes with very clear whites, a stiff mass of curls the non-colour of straw. She lived locally and seemed to spend all her time at the stables, although I suppose she must have gone to school. It was impossible to imagine Karen compliant in a classroom; her independent competence seemed so sealed and completed.

Karen was in charge by herself that Saturday morning when I arrived, busy in the middle of mucking out. She had taken the ponies down to the field. Wiping sweat from her forehead onto her sleeve, she frowned at me as if she could hardly recognise me: I wasn't supposed to emerge into her universe of the stables until hours and hours later. And she must have registered that I appeared for the first time without my mother, though she didn't comment. I babbled something about wanting to come up early, to help out – a motive Karen could take in and approve. She swept me with her focussed, narrow glance, summing me up, deciding to tolerate me.

– You can help with this lot.

She handed me one of the stiff brooms we used to clear the filthy pissed-on and shat-on straw out from the stalls. I didn't have my stable clothes on but in the abandonment of today it didn't matter. With Mum's money, I had bought chocolate and an orange drink at the shop across the road from where the bus stopped, so I wasn't hungry any longer; I set to work energetically. Soon I stripped off my jumper. Karen and I settled down into a companionable unspeaking rhythm of labour and procedure. I loved the noise of the bristles, hissing against the cobbles in the wet from the hose. The forbidden nursery stench was gagging, overwhelming; there was a triumph in getting so deep into muck, then resurfacing into an order where all the stalls were spread with clean straw, and all the hay-nets full. We didn't call what we cleaned up 'shit' or 'piss'. I suppose as little girls we were excited by the pony's shame-lessness, which was also innocent; and by the matter of fact way we were thrust up against their gargantuan bodily function, cheerfully chaffing and scolding them for it. We couldn't help seeing the male ponies' penises, sometimes extended in arousal – the older girls joked about their 'willies', though I never did, but joking couldn't encompass the naked enormity, appalling, stretching imagination and inhibition. Sometimes as you led the ponies back into a stall where you'd just put out clean bedding, they pissed into it voluptuously; we would groan and jeer, frustrated but also half delighted.

We must have worked for a good hour, then Karen made us instant coffee and I shared the rest of my chocolate with her. I'd never actually drunk coffee before, but I didn't say so, I told her I took three sugars; I was confusedly happy to see her stirring for me, there in the pavilion whose light was always heavy with dust motes, the inner sanctum of the stable-cult. From time to time I was visited by the knowledge that trouble waited for me at the end of this interlude of escape. No one knew where I was. I had begun something catastrophic when I slipped out of the routines of our life, to act by myself. I knew without think-ing about it that what seemed plain to me – my dereliction's existing in counter-balance with my mother's – would never for one moment be admitted or discussed by her. But I wasn't sorry, I was exulting, even though in my chest I felt a pain of postponed anxiety like a held breath. I didn't try to picture the scene in the bedroom, I stopped at the closed door. In my mind the door itself became a hieroglyph, expressing an unknown dread.

*

Karen began to open up to me, complaining about Jilly and Budge. Jilly had been supposed to help with the mucking out, but there was still no sign of her. – Sleeping it off, Karen said contemptuously. We went together to fetch the ponies up to the paddock, ready for the morning's classes to begin; as we strolled, she ripped off bits of wild clematis and sticky burs, lashing with them at the hedge in her indignation, rousing flurries of dust and papery moths. The air was warm and stuffy. The field was at the back of a new housing development; I had some inkling even then that this was not the real, deep countryside, but something scruffy and indeterminate, washed up like a residue around the edge of the city.

I didn't mistake Karen's confidences for friendship – she would have unburdened herself to whoever was there. She was also the sort of talker who didn't bother to fill you in on the background to what she was discussing, so that in order to follow her I had to make great leaps of imagination and comprehension through a dense web of particular detail: dates and times, things done and words spoken, disputed interpretations of what had been promised. Her grudges were obscure and passionate. Budge she seemed to tolerate ('He knows what's going on and doesn't like it'), but Jilly was 'two-faced' and 'could be a right cow'. She dramatised their duologues, ventriloquising Jilly's words in an exaggeratedly posh accent. 'I'm not very happy with your attitude Karen'. In these duologues Karen's clinching and flattening ripostes left Jilly lost for words. I gathered that Jilly was leaving more and more of the work at the stables up to Karen, paying her sometimes, but not on any agreed or regular basis. Sometimes she didn't even turn up for the classes and Karen had to take them.

– They've got me in a cleft stick, Karen said. – Because I love the horses, I won't leave them.

Of course I had imagined the world of the stables as a happy cohesion. Karen's revelations were wrenching for me, but also seemed an inevitable part of the initiations of this morning; I braced myself and grew into them. When we opened the gate to the field the ponies lifted their heads from where they were cropping grass. I thought they looked at us with patient regret and I felt a pang at our intrusion, but I knew better than to say so. Karen would think that was soppy; you wouldn't have known that horses were her life, unless you watched her carefully. She wasn't tentative or tender, as I was; she spoke about them as if they were comical, exasperating, a trial to be got through. But in the field they tolerated her approach when she came coaxingly towards them at an angle, holding the bridle out of sight behind her, making encouraging chirruping noises; whereas they wouldn't let me get anywhere near them. She told me to ride Dozey up to the paddock; she would ride Chutney, leading Star, and we would go back for the others.

We mounted at the stile. I had never ridden without a saddle before, but as with the coffee I didn't say anything. Dozey was the smallest of the ponies, only about eleven hands. Putting one hand on the withers where Karen showed me, I pivoted awkwardly up over the slippery broad barrel of his back, hanging on there, head down, gripping the halter for a moment – then trying to copy Karen's movements, swinging my leg across, heaving myself upright. I was hot in the face, knowing her assessing eye was on me. Because of her closed, blinkered perspective, it was easy to think that she wasn't noticing you, but in fact nothing escaped her.

– Grip harder with your knees, she advised offhandedly, as if my incompetence were only a thing of the passing moment. – Sit up straight. Relax. You can do it.

Tears stung in my eyes, wrung out by the great kindness of her condescension. When Karen took the classes, she was scathing. And I relaxed, I found my equilibrium. I felt the ponies muscle and sinew moving under mine, I breathed his smell as if we were one hot flesh.

*

So it was that I came riding into the yard at the very moment my mother made her appearance at the stables (she probably didn't even notice I was bareback). I think that I must have first turned up there at about nine – she arrived just before eleven, when morning lessons started. I saw her climb out of the passenger seat of a maroon-coloured car parked beyond the yard gate; she was wearing her heels, unsuitable in the mud, and her coat was hanging open with the silk scarf loose inside around her neck. She made an impression subtly different to the usual one, when she had toiled up with me on two buses: today she looked womanly, commanding and perfumed. At the same moment Jilly appeared out of the pavilion in wrinkled slacks and polo neck, sour-faced, dishevelled, hair scrunched in an elastic band, cigarette dangling off her lip. She raised an eyebrow in mild surprise at the sight of me on Dozey (her eyebrows were plucked to nothingness and had to be drawn back in brown pencil), but didn't comment.

– Take the ponies through into the paddock, Karen, she drawled around her cigarette, as if she'd been in charge of the whole operation from the beginning.

I half expected Karen to expostulate, breaking out with her grievances. But she only clicked her tongue at Chutney and rode on, her face closed like a surly, suffering boy's. Jilly unplugged the cigarette in a way she had, with a light popping noise, extending her free hand to my mother and putting on the caramel baritone charm she kept for parents. She obviously couldn't remember my mother's name. (I expect she found my mother beneath consideration, a prole. But she needed her money. And Mum would have been thinking Jilly looked 'a fright'.) Mum spoke in her most stand-offish, stilted public manner. Of course she didn't make a scene about my being there, she never would. She saved the scene for later, in private.

– Come on Stella, she said briskly, as if her collecting me had been planned all along. Awkwardly I slithered down from Dozey, landing somehow on my bottom on the cobbles. – Look at the state of you. I'm going to have to find something for you to sit on.

And we made our way to the maroon-coloured car.

Where in the driving seat a man was waiting.

*

Mum had called round at Nana's at about half nine, and no one had answered the door. Nana was inside (Mum had a key), but she had suffered a stroke. 'A slight stroke', Mum said decisively, as if she was tidying it away. Uncle Frank had taken Nana to hospital. (So that was why I hadn't heard Nana, when I woke up. Unless – this haunted me for a while – she'd had the stroke because she found me missing. Nana recovered, but she was never her old indefatigably busy self, she meandered into troughs of bewildered absence. She died when I was fourteen.)

Mum had guessed immediately where I might have gone.

We never once spoke of the possibility that I had come home first, and been inside the flat where she was sleeping, not alone. She never asked about the money I had taken, although she must have noticed it was missing, in that time when she had to count every penny. (I hid what was left of it at the bottom of my treasure box, spending it gradually on sweets.) A few days afterwards, when I was reading one evening on my bed, she came in and opened her hand, showing me the coral button and diamanté buckle.

– Are these yours?

I had forgotten about them. There had been too many other things to think about.

– Yes, I said. -I found them on my way home. On the bombsite.

– Pretty, she said. And gave them to me.

That was all.

'Buttons' was written to stand as an independent story, but it's also the second in a series of stories from Stella's life which may come together eventually as a novel. The first Stella story, 'Honour', will be published in *The New Yorker*.

POETRY

EMMA McGORDON

A father like me

I didn't want to be daddy's little girl,
I wanted to be daddy's son, I wanted a football,
a racing track, a power-car, a gun.

I didn't want Sindy, Polly Pocket, Barbie, I staged
a late night heist, a hit and run involving Ken
and that white Ferrari, Barbie's dead and Ken's
to blame, the Ferrari's in the car wash,
that was my kind of game.

I'd hold Sindy upside-down swirling her hair
in a puddle. *What you doin?* I'd hear him shout,
but I'd fight off my father's offer of a cuddle.

One Easter all trussed up – pink frill dress,
shiny new shoes, straw bonnet hat – I went exploring,
ribbons unravelling in the wind, I went
looking for my reflection in a bucket of oil,
its silky surface I swirled with a stick
never finding the bucket's bottom
only that pink and black don't mix,
each fingerprint spread as I tried to wipe the last.

Oil became a thing between him and me,
I grew up, bought old bangers of cars
learning measures made by a dipstick,
that everything with a yellow cap in a Ford
could be filled up; oil, water, washers,
ignoring my mother's new shade of pale pink lipstick.

I held my body rigid as he taught me to check tyres
and water, levels and tread, my back's axle aching.
When I pulled out the fuse for the wipers
instead of the flip catch for the bonnet
he made a comment about women and cars
and my heart was punctured.

He took my sister's boyfriend to the scrap yard
searching for spares, as the car turned the corner
of our road, I was left a part
only a front door key on my fob,
to him I was still his little girl,
he wanted me to meet a nice lad, settle down,
have babies I suppose.

He doesn't know of the army pants in class 3's
dressing up box, shoving them over my skirt,
he, my father, doesn't know that I was always the dad
while other girls fought over clip-on earrings and
dragged five-sizes-too-big heels across the orange
carpet, their toes in the points of 1986 stilettos,
I was busy being like him, rolling paper
pretending it was a cigarette, sitting in the chair
watching the news on a cardboard telly,
he didn't know I'd spent years basing myself on him.

Suddenly I find I've grown up all wrong,
Oedipal instead of Electra, got my wires crossed,
circuit board fused, systems shorted.
I was a physics paper problem where you decide
to close AB or DD to get EE, the lighthouse
to light so the boat can see sea.

My walk his, my talk his,
my voice an echo arguing with his,
for years I abandoned him,
too busy being my own version of him,
until I meet this woman who tells me
I'm not him, I'm me and that's fine.
For the first time I notice as I change gear
my hand actually does look like a woman's.

And this woman says having crossed wires
is a good thing – she finds them interesting
and this woman comes to know in me
something I never knew existed
this woman teaches me
to know my father as myself.
So, now each year, as we all grow older,
I find I do want to be my father's daughter.

INTERVIEW

SEEING ISN'T NECESSARILY BELIEVING

In Conversation with Terence Davies

Liverpool filmmaker Terence Davies is a great artist in what has been called 'memory realism'. He began in the 1980s a style of filmmaking which has become associated with ideas about memory: how we remember the past, and how we visualise our emotions. His most recent film *Of Time and the City* marked his return to Liverpool, the city of his birth, and has attracted much critical praise; it was rapturously received at Cannes film festival, had its UK premiere in Liverpool in 2008 at the Philharmonic Hall, and won the New York Critics' Prize in 2009.

The central theme that runs through all your Liverpool films is memory. The trilogy, Distant Voices, Still Lives, The Long Day Closes *and of course* Of Time and the City, *all these films are about memory, as if from the very beginning of your filmmaking days you are trying to capture the essence of memory.*

It's quite by accident. I didn't know I was doing that. You never do. You perceive something and you try to make the record as close to the memory experience as you can, to capture the same intensity. There were things that had huge effects on me that I didn't realise at the time. I just *looked* all of the time, I listened. That was natural to me. I remember even as a child going out and looking at the street and thinking: 'I've got to remember the way it looks today'. Certain things that have little or no importance at all suddenly take on huge meaning. I remember when I was about ten there was a big criminal trial running at the time. Devlin and Burns, a murder case. Rose Heilbron was the defence barrister and I remember them saying on the radio she was given leave to walk before the Jury. Why I should remember that God only knows. But the following Sunday everyone was listening to *Family Favourites*. In reality these two events were not connected but in my mind the ellipsis between the two made a 'true' memory from a 'false' one. It was a really lovely warm Sunday, all the doors were open; I could hear Jo Stafford singing 'See the Pyramids Along The Nile'... and I don't know why I remember that moment, the sheer intensity of it. When I was eighteen we got our first television, and over four nights on prime-time television Alec Guinness read the whole of the *Four Quartets* from memory. I was knocked out by it. I didn't understand a word of them but I thought I've got to read them. And I read them and they are my templates, along with the sonnets of Shakespeare and the music of Bruckner – I could not live without them.

But the point of memory is that it is cyclical, it is not linear. When memory's done badly it always *seems* linear. It's not, it's associative. In my childhood, when I was at my primary school, which was at the bottom of Edge Lane, we had a little patch of green which we were not allowed to play on. And it used to get cut in the summer and every time I smell cut grass I think: I'm back in Edge Lane all those years ago. And I can walk through that school now, I can walk through my house now, I can walk through those places that I went to watch movies. There were eight cinemas within walking distance of my house, and another eight in town. Every one was different. I remember where I saw particular films, where I sat, and I could even remember – if I saw it twice – whole shafts of dialogue and the images. I thought everybody did that because when my sisters went into the movies they came back and talked about what the story was. But, I didn't realise this at the time, they tell you what they *think* they saw. And that's the real magic. The other great piece of magic is that you have to experience films collectively, in the dark, but because of its power everyone feels like the secret is *only* being told to them. And that's what film is, that is the nature of memory, and you remember those things with such intensity.

But the down side is that I tend to live in the past. There's got to be change – if there's no change things ossify – but I feel unsafe when even little things change. My father was extremely violent. And I only made this mistake once – I was five and I ran into the house and I made a noise and he kicked me from one end of the house to the other. And I thought ah! I won't make that mistake again. But it made me supersensitive to changes of nuance. If I go into a room I can tell you who's had a row, or who is on edge.

The anthropologist Mark Ozer has written on memory and oblivion. He says that in order to remember you need at the same time to forget. A lot of the memory sketches you evoke are very personalised, localised and subjective.

Even with an autobiographical story you have to change things, because the narrative drive will tell you what it wants. Even if you do it exactly as you think it happened, the narrative drive will change, because once

TERENCE DAVIES

©Jack Taylor

you've shot it, it takes on a completely new life, and you have to listen to that *new* life. You give a little and then say: you've got to wait. You've got to wait till it's explained, and that's exactly what music does. A theme or an image might never be repeated but you never forget it and then, once it's been explained it's like listening to a musical resolution: Ah, *that's* what I've waited for. So you change the details of memory in order to make a narrative lie into a truth (which it really is) that you thought you experienced. And that's when it's fabulous; it takes on its own life. I remember my first film was *Singin' in The Rain* at the Odeon, and I wept all the way through it. My sister said, Why are you crying? And I said: They look so happy. My father had died and it had all been miserable but then we began to live. I think it was probably relief really.

How do you choose the music to go with your memory?

The songs are easy, because everybody sang them; everybody had their own particular song. My mother always sang 'I Get The Blues When It's Raining'. But often the practical difficulty is whether you can afford the copyright. In *Of Time and the City* I wanted Peggy Lee. I love that song; it's as great as anything by Schubert. I wrote a long letter saying: please let us use this, I loved it since I was a boy and then on the very last day we were cutting the film they said yes.

Don Boyd, who was helping us said, you won't get clearance for the Eliot because Eliot didn't like the cinema and he didn't want his poetry used. I thought, Oh God, what do I do? But I remembered a film that was on about fifteen years ago that John Betjeman wrote called *Bird's Eye View* – about Britain seen from the air – and he'd used part of the *Four Quartets*. Again I had to write a letter saying this is some of the greatest poetry in English, please can I use it, they said yes.

Another strong feature in all your films seems to be the rhythms of the day, the rituals and routines that punctuate the day. On the one hand these seem to set up entrapment – they're very rigid, very structured, but on the other I get the sense that you view these everyday domestic routines with a great deal of affection.

They give a great deal of solace and support. On a Saturday my brothers went to the match, and they got back at twenty-to-five. My mother had already made the pea soup, ready for them; they'd listen to the football results, which I listened to only for the rhythms of the lines. (I couldn't care less about football.) Your day was structured. You got up and my mother always put on the home service first, which was always the shipping forecast. Again I had no idea what it meant. But I thought it was mesmeric! They said things like: Fair Isle, Cromarty, Forties...Winds freshening from the South-East. Moderate to poor visibility. With some fog banks. And I'd be thinking isn't it erotic! And then you'd go to school and come home, and if it was later on in the year, there would be toasted potato cakes in front of the fire. Oh God that was heaven! I hated Thursday because that's when you had to go to the wash house. And we only had one set of curtains so the house looked too bare and it was hard work in those wash houses. But these were all those things that you did and you loved because it was very comforting! This was also reinforced by the church. You went to Sunday Mass, you went on holy days of obligation, and you went on Saturday to have your confession heard. When I said my first confession – those days you made it in the dark – I went down on my knees saying 'Pray Father give me your blessing' and he said, 'I'm over here!' I'd made my first confession to the central heating system.

The Trilogy *has your most raw and exposed work about sexuality and religion. Was making these films a response to depression or guilt?*

I came from a large Catholic background. I was a very devout believer; on one occasion I knelt and prayed literally until my knees bled. My last book-keeping job was in Birkenhead, so I had to go on the ferryboat at 8:15 in the morning and very often I sat and cried because of the sheer terror of never, never being able to get away from one's sexuality. This is why I'm celibate, I hate being gay. It's completely ruined my life. You can confess everything except the one sin that hovers over you. There's nothing worse than that kind of desperation. And it was true despair. The other part of it was quite practical: I hated working in accountancy even though I was really good at it. I applied to drama schools in London, but I never got into them – I hated London at the time; I was overwhelmed by it, and then I got into one in the Midlands; it wasn't a very good drama school but at least it got me out of accountancy. I couldn't go through that time again. My teens were ruined. I felt guilty all the time. It was the constant sense of being outside of God's grace. And I really did want to be like everybody else. I wanted to be like the rest of my family.

When I left school in 1960 I went into a shipping office for a year. The clerk who was over me was eighteen, and I felt he was terribly sophisticated, because he went out to the cinema and he noticed the photography. I felt that there was something odd about him, and then one night, the second week I was there, I said, 'I'll make some tea before we go close the office'. He said: 'I'm queer'. I said: 'Yes, I am too'. I thought at least there's one other person in the world.

When I went to secondary school I was beaten up every day for four years. It destroyed any kind of self-esteem. Of course, I thought I sounded like everybody else – all my family have strong Liverpool accents, but actually I sound like the Queen Mother! I have an imitative ear. I used to love listening to people with good voices. There was a wonderful woman on Radio 3 called Patricia Hughes, voice like Brahms, and I think I imitated her. I gave a lecture at Cambridge a very long time ago, and all these nineteen year-olds who were all going into the city said: 'Which university did you go to?' I said: 'Guess'. They said, Yale or Harvard because of the flat A. I said, 'No, I didn't go to any university. I have a flat A and a glottal G because I come from the north of England' – and it all went quiet. I thought I've peed on the chips there!

What are the individual things about Liverpool that you did find solace in and that you remember with affection?

My mother, every Christmas, she used to borrow £25 from the Leigh and Lend – she had to pay back over the year – the payback was £26.50, and she was absolutely terrified of missing a payment. The building was just off Dale St. As we walked past the George's Hall I used to look up and read *Artibus Legibus Consiliis* and I thought it was so strange and wonderful. I didn't know what it meant because I don't speak Latin. It's things like that I love, the little nooks and crannies. But really, *The Trilogy* isn't *about* Liverpool, it's about what it feels like when you feel that you're no longer in God's grace.

What comes across in Of Time and the City *in particular, but really in all your films is that they are lonely – it's an interior landscape.*

Yes I think they probably are, although I do think the first two are quite clumsy. In *Death and Transfiguration* I think I found my voice. It was because of Doris Day. When I grow up I want to be Doris Day. There's a wonderful song called 'It All Depends On You' in *Love Me or Leave Me* and it's just her voice and piano accompaniment; she has such a pure voice and I just thought if I juxtapose that with a funeral it will work. I didn't know why but I knew it would work. But one of the governors at school – because that was my graduation film – stood up behind me and said: this should never have been made.

The structures in your films lay out a very disciplined life. There are big differences in terms of growing up in the fifties and in the sixties, which brought a kind of freedom. And yet in your films the sixties don't exist – even though it's a period in Liverpool's history that is celebrated.

I grew up towards the end of the great American song book. Cole Porter was still writing in 1956, *High Society*, so I was used to that kind of writing, and I then discovered classical music which was a huge revelation to me. Mahler and then Shostakovich and Sibelius – these were revelations. I remember in 1956 my sister took me to see *Jail House Rock*, and I cringed throughout the whole of it. I thought doesn't he look ridiculous, he's got this awful voice and awful songs. And then The Beatles came along and they were even worse. I just couldn't bear them, I still can't. But what was true, walking around the city in the early 1960s there was an electricity in the air. I did love that. But I was changing too. Life was restricted, certainly in the fifties; if anybody had a posh accent you listened to them, and if they were in authority you automatically did as you were told. Things were expected of you. I remember when I went into the accountancy practice I would always rewrite my figures and underline them in red so it was perfectly lovely and tidy. My boss said: 'Why do you do it this way, Terence?' And I said: 'I can't do it badly. I'd feel guilty if I did it badly.' But in that restriction there was a kind of comfort because you knew where you were. You also knew your place which was *not* right. But you *felt* that you knew that things were constant, and not changing all the time. In change I feel as though I've got no ground on which to build anything.

The use of music seems to be something that comes from your imagination before you realise it in film. Do you work from music to the vision do you think, or from vision back to the music? Is there a specific process?

No. The shot is either written with that specific music in mind, or I write something and then think, Oh it needs something, and then I find it or I remember something that will work but it has to be instinctive. I grew up in the great period of American musical, *Singin' in the Rain*, *It's Always Fair Weather*, *Love Me or Leave Me*, *Calamity Jane*, *Pyjama Game*, the list is endless. When you're a child you absorb the world. I remember going to the Majestic at the bottom of Prescot Street to see *Pyjama Game*, Doris Day with this turtle neck sweater and this pencil thin skirt and white overall, and you think, God! That's a star. You should have that frisson when you love things. I go less and less to movies now. I won't sit through violence, I just can't. I had enough of that as a kid.

You describe Of Time and the City *as a visual poem rather than as a documentary. I'm interested in the relationship between cinema and poetry and how you see the two interplaying with one another. Are there any sort of commonalities in terms of grammar, in syntax between the two media?*

There's different syntax, but they have similarities. A poem is distilled down to its absolute essence, but it's the same with cinema. It can be a small thing in a not very good film. Very often you learn a lot from bad films. And those of you who want to make films – watch a lot of them. There's always something that's good. There's a not very good film made at the end of the 40s called *Carrie*, based on the Theodore Dreiser novel, with Jennifer Jones and Laurence Olivier. He's a married man, and he ruins his life socially. She becomes a stage star, and he ends up a beggar. She's appearing at this theatre, and he's in the alley and he asks for 25 cents. She recognises him and makes him come into the theatre with her; she takes him into the dressing room, but she's called to go on stage. He sits down on her dresser and there's money there. He takes exactly 25 cents. He gets up and goes to the door and at the door there's a gas ring. He switches the gas ring on – all you hear is sssssssssssss – and slowly he switches it off. And that's poetry.

What is your most treasured memory and what's your most hated memory?

My most treasured memories are all concerned with my mother. It's a very tiny thing but I can't watch it when it comes on the screen, in *The Long Day Closes* she's ironing. I just think I'll never see her again. The thing I hate most is the way we were treated by my father. He died of stomach cancer at home over two years, and it was awful. I had to sleep in the bed that he died in because my mother had no money. I hope that I've inherited some of my mother's stoicism – not in the strict sense of denying everything, but in the sense of taking what you are given in life and trying to do the best you can with it. She was full of love.

Was your father naturally cruel or was it just within the context of the family?

He was psychotic. His two brothers were equally disturbed, and there were two sisters who were disturbed. Only Auntie Anne – who lived in Angelsark Street – was lovely. But if you put it in a film nobody would believe it. His brother Peter would get very drunk and he only ever sang one song – 'Some of these Days' but sung with this kind of psychotic rage: 'Some. Of. These. DAYS. You're. Gonna. Miss Me HONEY'. Terrible! And the other nutter was Uncle Ted – he'd come in and he'd switch the light off and say [high pitched voice] 'I've switched the light off. I don't know whether I'm doing it right or wrong'. I can't forgive the infliction of cruelty. If you're not going to love your children, don't have them, and in those days if you made a bad marriage, there wasn't even a separation or a divorce, you had to stay with that person. But after my father died that house became like a magnet. Everybody came. It was wonderful. The most wonderful memory, apart from my mother, is Friday nights. My sisters used to have their friends come round. They would iron their underskirts with the flat irons, and all they had for make up was pan stick, majestic red lipstick and majestic red nail polish, 'Evening in Paris' scent and 15-denier nylons, in American tan. It was magical. I miss that more than anything else. I used to love Fridays.

But I must say not everybody likes my films – there was a question I answered one time – someone jumped up and asked: 'Why are your films so bloody slow and depressing?' I said: 'It's a gift'.

THE POET ON HIS WORK

ON 'ROULETTE'

Richard Meier

After a forgettable meal on the first night of a short break in Le Touquet, my wife and I wandered aimlessly through the streets, kicking ourselves that we'd done so little homework on a place that turned out to be a sort of poor man's Miami catering mainly for the British golfing market. Still, not to be defeated, we thought we'd enter into the 20s spirit of the place and try our luck at the Grand Casino.

In vitro fertilisation (the journey we would be embarking upon the following week) is – and here's an understatement – a sapping process, and its sapping qualities are felt long before the actual activities it entails begin. There's a heartsink moment when you admit that it's your only option, and perhaps the visit to the casino was all part of a rather elongated, if forlorn, attempt to rally our spirits. But with an excruciatingly limited budget – the croupier went clockwise around the table changing 200 euro notes into chips before I brought up the rear with my solitary, puny 20 euro bill – it wasn't exactly a Henry V moment.

I think it was on my final, or maybe penultimate, play that the rouletteness of the IVF process dawned on me, and with it the realisation – that all too rare thing – that there was a poem here. The similarities between roulette and IVF don't seem particularly strained after all: the stakes involved (emotional and financial), the fact of the winning and the losing, the way that the loss prevents one carrying on (financially of course but, in the case of IVF, genetically as well), the indifference of chance (the wheel of fortune etcetera), the drawn-out nature of the process (the ball taking an age, it can seem, to drop into its final numbered slot, the tortuous nature of IVF with its endless appointments, injections, invoices and upsets before the emperor's thumbs up or thumbs down). And there are others of course: the fact that gambling and making babies are activities which should only be undertaken by adults over a certain age. And that, so the voice of experience has it, both are a mug's game...

Sometimes I write poems which could benefit from a bit more space I think. A little more pause required, more poise. If 'Roulette' works as a poem however, that is probably in part down to rather breathless enjambment as the bets become increasingly desperate and my mind begins to run on to the real do-or-die moment, faintly ridiculous in the mundanity of its setting in the bathroom's cold, white spaces. A moment of potentially huge emotional, cultural, gendered and genetic fulfilment, or its opposite, and a kind of death. Looking back on the poem, I suppose that it is a kind of death encapsulated by 'fuck, red again' – which is, after all, pretty much the repeated experience of the couple for whom the dearly-wanted baby – regular as clockwork – fails to make an appearance.

I am a great admirer of Kate Clanchy's poetry, and I think that her collection *Newborn* marvellously captures the excitement and trepidation of bringing, or trying to bring, a new life into the world. Men don't write about this kind of stuff that much I feel, though I'm not really sure why. Perhaps it is because a man's role in pregnancy and birth remains – despite the NCT's laudable attempts to make it otherwise – somewhat that of the helpless bystander. IVF brings that powerlessness even more sharply into relief, and earlier. I wonder if my attempt to 'read' the pattern of the last ten goes of the roulette wheel was a stereotypically male attempt to impose some notion of control, however delusional, onto the proceedings, perhaps simply for my benefit, but perhaps also to attempt to reassure my wife that it was somehow in my gift to make things turn out alright in the end. Perhaps the writing of the poem – written of course before we knew the outcome – was also part of that same impulse.

As I was writing 'Roulette' I wondered about the slackness of the rhyme, the looseness of its general construction. On balance, however, it seemed injurious to meddle in this case. After all, the rhymes, however irregular and slant, help the poem cohere, and the iambic metre hopefully conveys something of the ineluctable quality of the whole process. Essentially though, this is a poem about things falling out, howsoever they may. As they will. As they did, in fact. I write this on holiday in Devon with my parents-in-law and my wife. And asleep in my wife's arms, our nine-week old daughter, Matilda. After all, it was a yes, a yes...

Roulette

Put it on a number, you smile, seeing
me eye the pattern of the last ten goes.
Funny to end up here, at the casino,
the first night of this break we can't afford,
but need, we feel, before the IVF... And so,

since nine of the last ten have been red, I plump
for black: first two chips (red though, damn), then four
(fuck, red again), now six (you've guessed it), then –
all in – our last eight chips, and watch the ball
race round and round the buffed wall of the roulette wheel,

so shiny I can see you, smaller, in
your long coat that could be a dressing gown,
and you emerging from the bathroom one month hence
to show me, by your face, that everything
is lost, or else not lost at all, but yes, but yes...

RICHARD MEIER

POETRY

RICHARD MEIER

Portrait of a woman in the first weeks of pregnancy

Not a study in consolidation.

But a woman holding out a slate before her,
a slate upon which sits a drop of mercury,
a drop that wants to stick together,
wants to come apart… A woman who

stands on a boat of some kind, running
at every pitch, scampering at every yaw,
to stop the drop from slipping, spilling,
lest, if it should fall, it would become
a million grief-filled molecules breathed in for ever more…

A woman who, after a good while of this,
is beginning to get the gist, to grin.

A woman who may even be dancing

Renunciation

Those times he feels his mother must be worried
he might say, to help, *That must be worrying…*

At others, should he sense an unsaid sadness,
he might venture, *That must be upsetting…*

And she will pause, then answer, *No, I'm not
the worrying type* or *Well, you can't change it,*

and then the namelessness that follows
a feeling going unacknowledged, swallowed.

Today though, as he left the hospital –
she was staying with his dad a little

longer – he felt as if a faith fell from him,
this gospel of his, of authenticity,

his mother there, alone and knowing it,
afraid, and feeling that too, the lift doors closing.

For a bridge suicide

From four, six, eight feet, maybe even ten,
water's a giving, all-embracing thing.

Above that, it begins to harden, starts
to slap, to frighten till by fifty or sixty

limbs get broken. Still, even at that height,
you feel if you just got your entry right

you could elicit softness, could slip in
and it would melt to kindness there and then…

And yet, there is a point, even so,
when water's transformation is complete,

a point at which the whole of the earth's surface
is uniformly unforgiving. As

she neared the top of the bridge's central stanchion
this was a point she recognised. And let go

CATHERINE
PICKSTOCK

STONES RING

THE MYSTERY OF THE SENSES

Catherine Pickstock

I n some contemporary thought, vision has been demonised. It has been associated with the gaze of commanding dominance of a subject over an object – a tyrannical gaze that appropriates the seen in terms of the inner demands or projections of the seer.

But this critique ignores the way in which sight, of all the senses, locates and is summoned by the particular. And it is the particular which holds our gaze not in a mode of dominance, but rather through the lure of fascination before the inexhaustibly specific.

The Victorian Catholic poet Gerard Manley Hopkins, somewhat under the influence of the scholastic philosopher Duns Scotus, referred to such a phenomenon as 'this-ness' and it is celebrated in all his verses. That which is seen in its 'this-ness' cannot be entirely commanded. Yet at the same time, that immediacy is paradoxically borrowed: it arrives from elsewhere. The immediate may be a sign of what lies beyond sight, a vision of the invisible.

In his Petrarchan sonnet 'As kingfishers catch fire', Hopkins commences with a vision of *haecceitas* or this-ness: the flashing kingfishers and the dragonflies who 'draw flame':

> **As kingfishers catch fire, dragonflies dráw fláme;**
> **As tumbled over rim in roundy wells**
> **Stones ring; like each tucked string tells, each hung bell's**
> **Bow swung finds tongue to fling out broad its name;**
> **Each mortal thing does one thing and the same:**
> **Deals out that being indoors each one dwells;**

Selves – goes itself; myself it speaks and spells,
Crying *Whát I do is me: for that I came.*

Í say móre: the just man justices;
Kéeps gráce: thát keeps all his goings graces;
Acts in God's eye what in God's eye he is –
Chríst – for Christ plays in ten thousand places,
Lovely in limbs, and lovely in eyes not his
To the Father through the features of men's faces.

Whereas the kingfishers spontaneously explode with their fiery selves, the import of such motion is already elaborated by the dragonflies who do not inaugurate but rather borrow the flaming element. By the end of the sonnet, this borrowing has become paramount: Christ, reflected in diverse limbs and faces, 'plays in ten thousand places', is 'lovely in eyes not his'. Hopkins's love for Christ – his sense of Christ in everything and everything in Christ – is a love for a Christ who is God incarnate.

For Hopkins, seen things express both themselves and an elsewhere, and in either case something in them always eludes our gaze even as we still see them. What is more, by expressing themselves they immediately shift from the mode of seen to the mode of heard: and so the poem passes almost at once from things seen but moving, to the transit of sounds: to the ringing of stones dropped into wells, the striking of the tongues of bells. Vision need not dominate; it naturally slides into the mode of the other senses and especially that of hearing. The primacy of vision, which causes it to be the most 'orientating' of the senses, ensures, through the mutation of sight into sound, taste, odour and touch, that an invasive strangeness lies at our very heart. So while each thing is locked into the 'indoors' (as Hopkins puts it) of 'thisness', it is also this interiority that it 'deals out' – like a cosmic card-shuffler. This speaking and spelling out of sound is also the way in which each thing 'goes', sustaining the journeys of the kingfisher and the dragonfly. In this way the visible is not lost in a nihilistic urge to be rid of what is too much desired, but is passed on anew, both seen and heard differently, so that the visible resounds. In being reconciled to the instantaneous passing of the object of sight – the scintillating flash of the kingfisher – the visible is restored to us in transmuted form as the audible: as flinging out broad its name.

That naming which goes on in his poetry is not merely static or separating but is in creative excess of literalism. Normally, when we organise the world around us, we imagine that certain elements are basic. We like to think that these elements can be counted, one by one by one, separately and bounded. But how do we know when we have seized hold of a countable thing? Do we always know when to determine that a thing has fully arrived and attained the estate of thinghood or this-ness? There can be pretenders to thingness. This is a human problem; our finite perspective is inclined to hold fast to things, shore them up, and enthrone the partial as if it were absolute. Blaise Pascal warned us not to hasten to conclude that a landscape is a lapidary edifice: 'A town or a landscape from afar off is a town and a landscape, but as one approaches, it becomes houses, trees, tiles, leaves, grass, ants, ants' legs, and so on, *ad infinitum*. All *that* is comprehended in the word "landscape"'. Antoine Arnauld and Pierre Nicole, in their Port-Royal critique of Descartes' sense of the separately countable, warned similarly: 'the smallest grain of wheat contains in itself a tiny world with all its parts – a sun, heavens, stars, planets, and an earth – with admirably precise proportions; […] there are no parts of this grain that do not contain yet another proportional world.' Why do we arrange things by assigning nouns which conceal their lineaments of time, agency, plurality and continuous aspect, fixing down momentarily the vicissitudes of things? Why do we enthrone a snapshot in the existence of a thing as the absolute arrival of a thing? Why do we classify and fix the manifold into the once-and-for-all? Why do we make things seem like neutral edifices when every arrangement includes an arbitrary moment of decision as to selection or de-selection? We reassure ourselves that words are neutral, that they *represent* reality and do not add to the world, but simply reflect

"Where the variousness of things is held down by detached words, we think we understand better the way things actually are. We forget it is all contrivance."

coolly its machinations. And words are especially seen as non-participants in the world when they are *written down and printed*: their apparent fixity, their detachment from the will of an individual, their occlusion of personal entailment or commitment or situatedness are dramatised.

Where the variousness of things is held down by the coolness of detached words, we think we understand better the way things actually are. We forget it is all contrivance. We forget the moment when we decided that we would count the contrivance as the real. And we are accordingly disquieted by those places distinguished by the unpredictable give and take at fraught boundaries; places where the assigning of names is disputed. In these places, we confront the real in all its multiform, situated, endlessly interpretable arrival.

But an encounter with Hopkins's poetry involves something other than such illusory fixedness: it involves circuits of connected energy, shifts of boundaries between words and between senses, new locutions in flux: 'roundy wells', 'stones ring', 'that being indoors'. One can con-clude that vision need not dominate, because it naturally slides into the mode of the other senses and especially that of hearing. When the thing speaks, we see at once its inviolable specificity and its mysterious auto-indication as being itself more than itself.

Christian tradition has frequently recognised this synaesthesic slide. It is for this reason that it did not, as some imagine, regard the visual as straightforwardly the most spiritual sense, in such a way that vision formed the bridge in a hierarchy between lower and external senses and higher and internal spiritual reflection.

Instead, in the major tradition stemming from Origen in the second century AD, the soul or 'heart' is allegorised in terms of all the senses, in such a way that every sense is regarded as being at once internally spiritual and externally physical. For this *schema* vision is not especially interiorising. Rather, it is involved in a different oscillating contrast: it allows us the greatest private 'grasp' of a sensed object, and yet also in-troduces us to the most silent and resistant aspect of the external thing which conveys to us its 'this-ness'.

Synaesthesia is vividly involved in the curious medieval tradition that concerned 'eating beauty' at the Eucharist. Whereas under ordinary circumstances, to 'eat beauty' would be to devour and destroy it, it was thought that in the taking of wine and bread at the Mass, we are partially assumed by the very beauty we consume, and so our own being is trans-figured and shines with a new inward and outer light. By a further process of synaesthesia, we are called upon in the Mass to 'taste and see', not first to see and then to taste, but through tasting literally to see further.

The idea of the 'spiritual senses', or the notion that there are psychic equivalents for physical sensations, and even parts of the body, is not only traceable to the Church Fathers but is rooted in the Bible, since

"Unless we see something with 'the eye of the mind', we will not see anything with our physical eye at all"

the Bible spoke of 'the heart' of a human being in a way that was both physical and spiritual, and included both thinking and willing, as well as suggesting a kind of concentration of the whole human personality. 'Sensing' has a dual aspect, outer and inner, from the very outset, in accordance with the double Biblical meaning of the term 'heart'. When we see something in the first place, we only see it because we simulta-neously imagine and grasp it to some degree with our minds. Unless we see something with 'the eye of the mind' from the outset, we will not see anything with our physical eye at all.

And if we see from the outset also with the inner eye, then from the outset we relate one mode of sensation to another. Our seeing dark trees against the far background of the setting sun is affected by our awareness that we can touch one, but not the other. And were it not for our sense of hearing, we simply would not see the organ in a Church as a musical instrument. The mysterious mental operation of synaesthesia is in play whenever just one of our physical sensations is at work. The Church Fathers sometimes spoke in synaesthesic terms when they declared that our eyes should listen, our ears see, or our lips attend like

"The possibility of this deepening is connected with the excess of material things over rational thought."

ears to the word of God through a spiritual kiss – suggesting that in our inner sense contemplation is also active obedience and *vice versa*, while all our speaking to and of God must remain an active attention to his presence. But, once again, this kind of language does not so remove us from our literal bodies, as one might think: instead, an inner and a synaesthesic response invades the surface of our skin in the course of our original sensitive responses.

Because sensation has an interior aspect from the outset, it becomes possible for this interior aspect to be deepened. However, the very possibility of this deepening is paradoxically connected with the excess of material things over rational thought. The mind can exceed abstract reflection in the direction of 'mystical' encounter only through the constantly renewed prompting of corporeal sensing by sacramental physical realities. The 'distance' of material things from us is a vehicle for conveying the infinite 'distance' of God from us. This sense of distance is most of all conveyed by sight, since it most of all amongst the senses sustains the 'over-there' character of the sensed object.

Hopkins' cosmically liturgical poetry involves all three aspects: synaesthesia, the excess of matter over itself, the obstinately homely and yet mysterious resistance of the ordinary seen reality. This triple density sets up circuits of connected energy, shifts of boundaries between words and between senses, new locutions in flux: 'roundy wells', 'stones ring', 'that being indoors'. In this way Hopkins' poetic worship is both internal and external, both sublimely elevating and yet materially earthed, while it ensures a circular communication through speaking, hearing, tasting, touching and smelling.

Thus after the rapid shift in the octet from the visible to the aural, the sestet invokes a figure who integrates all the senses and moreover integrates inner with outer sensation. This is the cosmic worshipper who is the 'just man'. Just as 'stones ring', and each thing 'Selves – goes itself', so likewise 'the just man justices'. And thereby he 'keeps gråce: that keeps all his goings graces'. His only way of 'keeping' grace, which cannot really as gift be kept at all, is to 'keep all his goings graces', to keep, in other words, by giving way and yet by sustaining this outgoing as itself gracious. This is what Hopkins calls the 'inscape' of 'this-ness', the unique grace of his way of doing things, of meting out justice. The mark of the specificity of a thing – like the character of the just man which is specific in the very unpredictability of the rightness of his decisions – is that it is inexhaustible. Thus the just man 'Acts in God's eye what in God's eye he is – ' And the dash permits us initially to take this line as complete in itself, and the verb 'to be' in the end as the sole predicate. The just man being just is just as he should be, already in time he is his eternal true self.

But after the dash there is Christ. For Hopkins, all particularities point beyond themselves towards Christ. For in 'sharing' in Christ as God, creatures also link through time and place to Christ's divine humanity. In being conjoined to this, as parts of the body of Christ, their singularity is fully sustained even as it fades into its own greater glory.

All like the dragonfly 'draw flame' from Christ, but that he himself goes with everyone else is implied by the ambiguous 'To' in the last line of the poem: 'To the Father through the features of men's faces'. It is God's creative eye that is supreme; but Christ's 'way back' is through the specificity of us all. The beckoning of sight by the thing, towards that thing, betokens what lies beyond that thing.

POETRY

MATT MERRITT

Winterbourne

Where summer daubed a broken promise
in every yellow, brown and green,
storm and season have thinned the trees
to a glint of running water
where no stream has been for years.
It is pooling across the lowest meadow
and forcing the sheep to the furthest corner,
bringing gulls down out of nowhere.
It is making a nonsense of our certainties,
making good on all the old maps,
explaining the fields, the hedges, the villages,
the line of the road, the meanders of this path.
They'd have you believe it rises only
in time of war, or plague or famine, or else
to herald great good fortune, but today
it means nothing beyond the turn
and turnabout of seasons, the muddy ubiquity
of water, and all its small insurgencies.

Sketches For A New Town
for James W Wood

I woke still walking through streets
wide with wonder, pennypacket parks
green with promise, the clean suburbs
speaking of a certain simplicity,
the protective geometry of straight lines
giving on to the fields of our future.

*   *   *   *   *   *   *   *

I have centred my designs
upon the highest point in our compass.
Not because the top
opens out some brave new vista;

instead it's how the climb
leaves no choice but to fill your eyes
with one patch of sky
and all its changes.

*   *   *   *   *   *   *   *

I have tried to envisage the scenes
in which the inhabitants might make
much of the raw materials of their days,

in which families arriving from
the overcrowded cities might raise
more than a little dust,

in which any man or woman
might leave their mind open
to the ice-blue lens of the evening air.

*   *   *   *   *   *   *   *

High ceilings, deep windows
and judicious use
of the pale local ironstone.
This is how we plan to hang on
to every precious grain of light.

*   *   *   *   *   *   *   *

You will notice we have framed her
between two north-south straights
that neither diverge nor draw together

      oblivious parallels

although projective geometry and the curvature
of planes says that, followed far enough,
they meet at the point known as a singularity.

*   *   *   *   *   *   *   *

Seen from here, the clean lines, the mirror-image squares,
the smooth crescents and the whole easy symmetry
might be supposed to represent a world in microcosm,
or else the symbol, or device, of our progress.

Consider this prospect, though. From this lower,
closer vantage, all that can be said for certain
is that one way opens onto another, at a point
somewhere just beyond our comprehension.

ARTIE SHAW

ESSAY

READING ARTIE SHAW

Brian Murray

elebrity at this moment,' wrote the American essayist Joseph Epstein in 2005, 'is epidemic, and it's spreading fast, sometimes seeming as if nearly everyone has got it. Television provides celebrity dance contests, celebrities take part in reality shows, and perfumes carry the names not merely of designers but of actors and singers. Without celebrities, whole sections of the *New York Times* and *Washington Post* would have to close down. So pervasive has celebrity become in contemporary American life that one now begins to hear a good deal about the phenomenon known as the Culture of Celebrity' – a culture that seems insatiably interested in all of the gossip and glitz that surround our modern demigods, those stars and 'icons' of the media age.

But of course there's something tinny about celebrity – something provisional and fake. Fame, we've long assumed, deservedly comes to gifted people whose actions or creations have real influence or enduring worth. Celebrity, however, suggests an ability to get yourself, somehow, amplified. Famous people belong to history. But celebrities are commodities contrived, hyped, and inevitably thrown away by the now ubiquitous forces of mass media and mass marketing. Andy Warhol was surely thinking of celebrity when, in the 1960s, he liked to say that soon everyone living would enjoy fifteen minutes of fame.

Artie Shaw is famous – a virtuoso clarinetist who, during the 1930s, 40s, and 50s, frequently broke new ground. As a bandleader, Shaw sold millions of records, including his innovative arrangements of 'Star Dust' and 'Begin the Beguine'. Shaw's 'Concerto for Clarinet' and similar compositions combined classical and jazz elements in an unprecedented manner; and his later, still fresh-sounding recordings with the Gramercy Five also helped inspire new directions for jazz in the years to come.

> *"Every note you could feel in his heart"*
> *–Ray Charles*

Long hailed as one of the Kings of Swing, Shaw also deserves credit as one of the progenitors of bebop. In fact, although he looked perfectly suave in a tuxedo, Shaw was always something of a provocateur. He was one of the first bandleaders to showcase a 'colored' singer, Billie Holiday, with his otherwise all-white orchestra – a musically astute move that was not warmly cheered when Shaw and the band toured the segregated American South. Ray Charles, for one, hailed the fact that Shaw 'had so much feeling in his notes. Every note you could feel in his heart. Artie Shaw was one of the greatest musicians that ever lived'.

But Shaw was also a celebrity who, in his prime, was barraged with the sort of fervid, sometimes hysterical attention that, we tend to forget, did not begin with the Beatles or even with Elvis Presley. Because much of the heavy machinery of the culture of celebrity was already in place during the 1920s, the handsome Shaw – born Arthur Arshawsky in 1910 to immigrant parents on New York's lower East Side – was from the start groomed and sold by skilled agents of mass publicity. Initially, at least, Shaw welcomed the glare, not only because he hoped to distance himself from the poverty that had cramped his parents' lives, but because from the age of fourteen he had worked without stopping toward his goal of musical success. As a struggling musician Shaw often felt 'on the periphery of life', waiting for recognition and steady work. 'I would stand', he later recalled, 'like Tonio Kröger, looking in at the dancers from his dark veranda, bitterly envious of the young lovers inside the warm, bright, music-filled room – but never able to break through and become a part of what he longed for so hungrily.'

Artie Shaw was also very probably the most literate pop star of the twentieth century, an ambitious and lifelong reader who published three books of his own, including two volumes of short stories and *The Trouble with Cinderella* (1952), a memoir infused with social and psychological themes. As a fiction writer, Shaw's talents were limited; he will never be confused with Theodore Dreiser, his first literary hero, nor even with Romain Rolland, whose *roman-fleuve, Jean-Christophe*, inspired Shaw's own long, unfinished, and apparently unpublishable autobiographical novel, *The Education of Albie Snow*. *The Trouble with Cinderella*, however, does hold up as a readable and distinctive postwar autobiography. It is full of prescient reflections on celebrity culture – even as it reminds us of how difficult it is for autobiographers, even those asserting their un-flinching candor, to be entirely perceptive about themselves.

In part, *The Trouble with Cinderella* offers the familiar narrative of the gifted but poor kid who works hard and hits it big. Shaw, who quit school at fifteen, turned to music after watching vaudeville shows in a local theater. He was especially impressed by one stage musician who wore a 'blue-and-striped blazer' and blew artfully into a shiny gold sax-ophone. Here, Shaw decided, was an agreeable way to make a living. So he bought a secondhand sax and practiced day and night, much to the annoyance of his father, a 'surly, disgruntled' man who disdained this obsessive interest in what, in Yiddish, he termed a 'blosser', or kazoo. But Shaw carried on, performing with local and travelling dance bands while, in his spare time, mastering the clarinet as well. Shaw was in a hurry, and by the time he reached his mid-twenties he had become a bankable star, shooting upward. Shaw's orchestra attracted top players, sold lots of records, and took bookings at Madison Square Garden in New York and other top venues. Shaw married Lana Turner, another star, and later Ava Gardner, aptly publicized as the most beauti-ful woman in Hollywood. Shaw, indeed, achieved his boyish dream of becoming a household name. He appeared regularly on radio's George Burns and Gracie Allen Show. He made a movie with Fred Astaire. At his peak he was making $60,000 a week when the average American salary was well under $2,000 a year.

In his memoir, however, Shaw makes no attempt to court favor with the men who ran the music industry during the heyday of his amazing career; they were nearly all, he implies, philistines with few creative instincts, their sole goal the manufacture of chart-toppers likely to generate great piles of cash. A good musician, Shaw liked to say, plays 'three chords for beauty's sake' for every chord he must play to pay the rent. From the start Shaw was deeply competitive (he liked to mock, as stolid, his great rival Benny Goodman), and he sought perfection as an instrumentalist who understood and supported serious music. Thus Shaw also performed, to critical acclaim, with philharmonic or-chestras. He recorded works by Shostakovich, Poulenc, and Milhaud. On one occasion, he even assisted in the financial support of Arnold Schoenberg, exiled in California during the Second World War. ('I saved

Schoenberg's butt', he liked to declare, in later years.) More and more it bothered Shaw that what the vast public demanded – and, of course, what really paid – were dance tunes and the 'hits' he repeatedly played. Indeed 'Artie Shaw', he came to believe, was himself a fictional character, a corporate brand name like Betty Crocker or Uncle Ben. The star called Artie Shaw clenched his teeth and, over and over again, ordered his orchestra to hop through 'Frenesi' and 'Begin the Beguine'. But meanwhile Arthur Arshawsky seethed, fearing that, at the end of the day, he would be known not as a great musician, but as just another show business celebrity.

Certainly, Arshawsky/Shaw never understood the sense of proprietorship that so many 'fans' direct toward 'highly publicized' names. 'All ordinary standards of behavior', he writes in *The Trouble with Cinderella*, seem to go by the boards'. 'There have been so many times over the past twelve or thirteen years when I have seen ordinary people behave in the most extraordinary way toward me, that I can only come to one conclusion – apparently there are two kinds of behavior in our society, both perfectly acceptable. One is called "manners", and it operates under ordinary circumstances. The other – well, that's the way you behave with people called "celebrities". Whatever the hell that is.' Shaw learned that, frequently, he could not stroll through the streets without a disguise. Restaurant meals were also difficult. He might be

"An audience is in many respects no more than a mob under loose control."
– Artie Shaw

sipping a tomato juice, say, or salting his potatoes, when quite suddenly a total stranger would appear, hovering at his table and demanding a kiss. Shaw, eventually, came to see himself as 'a sort of side-show freak'. He also developed a 'near paranoiac kind of behavior' after realizing that 'the audience which roars its approval of the successful performer at one moment can at the very next turn on the same performer and practically rend him limb to limb. For an audience is in many respects no more than a mob under loose control.' '$ucce$$', in Shaw's spelling, was not what it was cracked up to be.

Shaw declines to discuss 'my entire clinical case history'. But he does admit to assorted neuroses aggravated by his endless exposure in the public eye. In fact, *The Trouble with Cinderella* reminds us that Freudian terms and assumptions were nearly obligatory in postwar American writing; that the spread of 'pop psychology' begins not in the 1970s but some twenty years before. Shaw, who was always tight with his praise, does extol his own extensive experience with psychoanalysis, claiming it helped him perceive how his own unsettled childhood with an angry, absent father and an emotionally controlling mother – a Freudian *tableau* if ever there was one – brought forth 'a terrible sense of insecurity coupled with an inordinate desire to prove myself worthy'.

For Shaw, finally, what mattered most was a life of the mind – a remarkable aspiration for a man who had dropped out of high school and who had read very little as a child. But by the time he reached eighteen, Shaw 'became a reader in earnest'. He 'went at this business of soaking up books with a persistence and determination and dogged tenacity that still astonishes me when I think about it'. He read constantly, if haphazardly, combing libraries and asking his better-educated colleagues for recommended titles. While living in New York, Shaw took extension classes at Columbia University in order 'to directionalize the pattern and scope of my reading'. He was interested in 'how all this stuff I was reading had got written in the first place. Who were these people who did the writing? Why did they do it? What made a man want to become a writer? And, of course, how did a guy go about it – how was it done?'

At one point, with his musical career in bloom, Shaw thought seriously of quitting it all and earning a Ph.D. He discussed his plan with a working professor, an 'excellent mathematician' who could not believe that any intelligent person, given the choice, would prefer teaching college students to tooting a horn for real money on a nightclub stage. 'You'll find yourself,' he warned Shaw, 'some twenty years from now, worrying about money, worrying about trying to meet your annual expenses on a salary no self-respecting plumber would be willing to work for. On top of that you'll be all snarled up with campus and faculty politics, disillusioned with teaching, because for every one student who wants to learn anything you'll run up against five thousand who are only there for the sake of the degree by which they hope to better themselves financially.' Sure, 'it's secure, as far as lives go. But it's a kind of living death, too.'

Shaw went back to his clarinet.

He did, however, quit performing for good in the 1950s and, with varying degrees of success, settled down to write. Shaw, who died, age ninety-four in 2004, continued to pursue difficult tasks in an obsessive way: in middle age his recreational activities included both championship target shooting and advanced mathematics. But he was also massively self-absorbed – 'the most selfish man that ever lived', as an exasperated radio producer who worked with the older Shaw once complained, an 'enormously narcissistic man in a cocoon'. Tom Nolan's recent biography – *Three Chords for Beauty's Sake* – tends to bear this out, and helps explain why Shaw's fiction, which is amusing enough in its way, lacks real distinction. Because he could not readily muster much interest in the lives and thoughts of others, Shaw was able generally to write about himself; to tell the tale, variously embellished, of 'the curious metamorphosis of a shy, introspective little Jewish kid named Arthur Arshawsky into a sort of weird, jazz-band leading, clarinet-tooting, jitterbug-surrounded Symbol of American Youth during an entertainment era characterized by the term "Swing".' The late screenwriter and novelist Budd Schulberg, who knew Shaw at the height of his popularity, did recall him fondly, for there 'was something very touching about the way he was so intellectually curious', reading furiously to discern the secrets of life. But Schulberg also recalled the times Shaw 'would stand with his back turned, and he would play these great solos, and he – wouldn't acknowledge the audience.' 'They were just – idolizing him! And he didn't give *them* the time of day.'

And so Shaw, who spoke famously of the pleasures of music, of hitting just the right notes in an inspired way ('better than sex', he liked to say), seems not to have fully grasped the full range of pleasures that can accompany a cultivated mind. He continued to read widely, well into old age; his final house, a California bungalow, was walled with books. But Dolan's book leaves one to gather that, perhaps particularly as he aged, Shaw read mainly to demonstrate the breadth of his erudition, to win arguments and bolster the opinions he had nursed for years. Alas he was largely unable to engage in amiable intellectual discussions with his friends and peers – apparently because, in the final analysis, he assumed that he had no peers. Such egotism undoubtedly served Shaw well as an ambitious bandleader – and probably would not have hindered him greatly had he, in fact, quit the music business, earned his Ph.D., and lodged himself, as Professor Arthur Arshawsky, behind a different sort of podium. Artie Shaw, as Ava Gardner remembered, 'never stopped talking'.

POETRY

PETER ROBINSON

Lawrie Park Avenue
by Camille Pissarro, 1871

Wisps of white cloud in a pale turquoise sky
Pissarro painted out-of-doors,
and a church spire, its creamy stone,
two or three passers-by.

He painted out one female figure.
Her pentimenti could be seen
still on the gravel, advancing towards me,
as a darker stain.

Sydenham in an early springtime
just over a century after,
not far from the hospice where she worked,
I could imagine finding us
on that avenue again.

Then here as warmth has come, at least,
there are things to do with the past –
like droplets on those steady leaves,
her Solomon's seal after rain.

And down by more leafage-filled gardens,
the flimsy petal, purple-hearted poppies
bring home illusions of another life's
occluded possibilities.

With foxglove, iris, the night-scented stock,
everything that didn't happen,
disappointed, went awry
is back as if making a mockery
of how it was, or why.

But lacking such things to do with the past,
like this figure he had painted out
who fills the air with an indelible stain,
there'd be no possibilities.

They thicken into leaf, his flanking trees.

Look, now, it's as plain as plain.

PETER ROBINSON

Edited by
ANGELA MACMILLAN

A Little,
ALOUD

'Reading aloud
is pleasure.
Pure pleasure.'
STEPHEN
FRY

With a foreword by
BLAKE MORRISON

To buy *A Little, Aloud* for the special price of £6.99 (Rrp £9.99), including free
UK p&p, call 01206 255 800 and quote the reference 'reader organisation'.

ALL ROYALTIES GO TO THE READER ORGANISATION

YOUR RECOMMENDATIONS

BOOKS ABOUT...
INDIA

Angela Macmillan

Mark Twain said 'India is the cradle of the human race, the birthplace of human speech, the mother of history, the grandmother of legend, and the great-grandmother of tradition'. It has sixteen official languages and a very ancient literary tradition. Each of the books below belongs to the more recent form of Indian fiction in English and represents something of the truth of India in the hundreds of truths that make up the unreachable whole. As recent bestsellers, the novels of Salman Rushdie, Vikram Seth, Arundhati Roy and Aravind Adiga do not need further promotion and are absent from the list. No doubt I will hear of more books that perhaps ought to be here but are not.

Ruth Prawer Jhabvala, *Esmond in India*
1958 (ISBN 978-0140052879)

While the author is well known for her collaboration with Merchant Ivory in such films as *Howards End* and *A Room with A View*, her wonderfully involving short stories and novels deserve a wider readership. *Esmond in India* brings 1950s' Delhi, so soon after partition, most vividly to life. The heat; the smells of cooking and bodies; the colours, are so real you can feel, taste, smell and see them. The characters are fully realised and you will care about them as they struggle through their daily lives, and with the conflicting values of a newly independent India.

R. K. Narayan, *The Painter of Signs*
1976 (ISBN 978-0140185492)

The setting for most of Narayan's short stories and novels is the fictional town of Malgudi in Southern India. In this short novel, Raman the sign writer, meets and falls hopelessly in love with Daisy, a forward thinking Indian woman with an almost ruthless mission to promote birth control in India. In pursuing his desire to marry her at all costs, Raman comes to realise the extent to which his old and deeply religious aunt has given her life to his every comfort and need. It is as if representatives of contemporary, modern and traditional India meet at an historical milestone and find their only way forward is in pursuit of their own individual courses. A funny, touching and insightful novel.

Paul Scott, The Raj Quartet
1966–71 (ISBN 978-1857152982)

Many will remember the iconic television version of the 1980s, *The Jewel in the Crown*. As this fades from memory, it is well worth revisiting the four novels: a heavy but worthwhile investment in reading time. During the last days of the British Raj in India, the lives of myriad characters are strongly evoked against what Scott calls the 'perpetually moving stream of history'. At the heart of the book, the failure and brutal consequences of the relationship between the English girl Daphne Manners and the Indian Hari Kumar, foreshadows the violent end to imperial rule in India in the tragedy of partition.

Khushwant Singh, *Train to Pakistan*
1956 (ISBN 978-0143065883)

In the immediate aftermath of the creation of the state of Pakistan, millions of lives were lost as people fled backwards and forwards across the new frontier in search of a place of safety, such as the remote village of Manro Majra; that is until a train load of massacred bodies arrives, unleashing a tidal wave of religious hatred between previously peaceful Sikhs and Muslims. Written ten years after the actual events, this is a chronicle of a terrible moment in history that is also a timeless narrative of racial and religious intolerance.

Jhumpa Lahiri, *Unaccustomed Earth*
2009 (ISBN 978-0747596592)

A bit of a cheat really as this collection of short stories is not about India but about the experience of Bengali immigrants in America as they struggle, in the pull of two continents and two cultures, to find their own place on the earth. Beyond this, however, the stories are connected by Jhumpa Lahiri's concern to show in the closest of all human relationships – parents and children; brothers and sisters; best friends – how the necessary distances between one human being and another, can so easily become unbridgeable gulfs. What is particularly fine about the title story is a daughter's realisation that despite her growing feelings of powerlessness in her life, she does have the ability to step back from the gulf and hold onto a new closeness between herself and her father.

Also recommended: the novels of Anita Desai and Rohinton Mistry.

OUR READ: LIVERPOOL READS JUST GOT BIGGER!

Due to the popularity of The Reader Organisation's annual reading campaign, Liverpool Reads is now bigger than ever, and has a new identity: **Our Read.**

Our Read is, like Liverpool Reads, a big book giveaway – we distribute thousands of free copies of one book to children and young people, encouraging them to read for pleasure. But in 2011 we will be able to send the book further a×eld, reaching schools, libraries, youth groups and high streets in destinations as diverse as Wirral, Bootle, Liverpool, London, Denmark, Melbourne, Mongolia and Sierra Leone!

The book, specially written for **Our Read** 2011, is *The Unforgotten Coat* by award-winning author and screenwriter Frank Cottrell Boyce (and it includes fantastic pictures from local photographer Carl Hunter). Thanks to Frank and Walker Books, we will have 50,000 copies to give away free of charge when **Our Read** launches on March 3rd (World Book Day).

We would love your support to help us reach those who would benefit most from the campaign. If you are in touch with a school, library or group that you think would like a set of books, please let us know by using the contact details below.

Charlotte Weber: charlotteweber@thereader.org.uk/ 0151 794 3849

HOW THE RHINOCEROS GOT HIS SKIN

Rudyard Kipling

Now that our book *A Little, Aloud* is published and out in the wide world, we would like to hope that more people will read aloud to one another, including readers of the magazine. To that end we offer here, as a continuation of books about India, one of Rudyard Kipling's *Just So Stories* for you to share with someone you care for. Go on; try it and see.

Once upon a time, on an uninhabited island on the shores of the Red Sea, there lived a Parsee from whose hat the rays of the sun were reflected in more-than-oriental splendour. And the Parsee lived by the Red Sea with nothing but his hat and his knife and a cooking-stove of the kind that you must particularly never touch. And one day he took flour and water and currants and plums and sugar and things, and made himself one cake which was two feet across and three feet thick. It was indeed a Superior Comestible (*that's* magic), and he put it on the stove because *he* was allowed to cook on that stove, and he baked it and he baked it till it was all done brown and smelt most sentimental. But just as he was going to eat it there came down to the beach from the Altogether Uninhabited Interior one Rhinoceros with a horn on his nose, two piggy eyes, and few manners. In those days the Rhinoceros's skin fitted him quite tight. There were no wrinkles in it anywhere. He looked exactly like a Noah's Ark Rhinoceros, but of course much bigger. All the same, he had no manners then, and he has no manners now, and he never will have any manners. He said, 'How!' and the Parsee left that cake and climbed to the top of a palm tree with nothing on but his hat, from which the rays of the sun were always reflected in more-than-oriental splendour. And the Rhinoceros upset the oil-stove with his nose, and the cake rolled on the sand, and he spiked that cake on the horn of his nose, and he ate it, and he went away, waving his tail, to the desolate and Exclusively Uninhabited Interior which abuts on the islands of Mazanderan, Socotra, and the Promontories of the Larger Equinox. Then the Parsee came down from his palm-tree and put the stove on its legs and recited the following *Sloka*, which, as you have not heard, I will now proceed to relate:—

> Them that takes cakes
> Which the Parsee-man bakes
> Makes dreadful mistakes.

And there was a great deal more in that than you would think.

Because, five weeks later, there was a heat wave in the Red Sea, and everybody took off all the clothes they had. The Parsee took off his hat; but the Rhinoceros took off his skin and carried it over his shoulder as he came down to the beach to bathe. In those days it buttoned underneath with three buttons and looked like a waterproof. He said nothing whatever about the Parsee's cake, because he had eaten it all; and he never had any manners, then, since, or henceforward. He waddled straight into the water and blew bubbles through his nose, leaving his skin on the beach.

Presently the Parsee came by and found the skin, and he smiled one smile that ran all round his face two times. Then he danced three times round the skin and rubbed his hands. Then he went to his camp and filled his hat with cake-crumbs, for the Parsee never ate anything but cake, and never swept out his camp. He took that skin, and he shook that skin, and he scrubbed that skin, and he rubbed that skin just as full of old, dry, stale, tickly cake-crumbs and some burned currants as ever it could *possibly* hold. Then he climbed to the top of his palm-tree and waited for the Rhinoceros to come out of the water and put it on.

And the Rhinoceros did. He buttoned it up with the three buttons, and it tickled like cake crumbs in bed. Then he wanted to scratch, but that made it worse; and then he lay down on the sands and rolled and rolled and rolled, and every time he rolled the cake crumbs tickled him worse and worse and worse. Then he ran to the palm-tree and rubbed and rubbed and rubbed himself against it. He rubbed so much and so hard that he rubbed his skin into a great fold over his shoulders, and another fold underneath, where the buttons used to be (but he rubbed the buttons off), and he rubbed some more folds over his legs. And it spoiled his temper, but it didn't make the least difference to the cake-crumbs. They were inside his skin and they tickled. So he went home, very angry indeed and horribly scratchy; and from that day to this every rhinoceros has great folds in his skin and a very bad temper, all on account of the cake-crumbs inside.

But the Parsee came down from his palm-tree, wearing his hat, from which the rays of the sun were reflected in more-than-oriental splendour, packed up his cooking-stove, and went away in the direction of Orotavo, Amygdala, the Upland Meadows of Antananarivo, and the Marshes of Sonaput.

THE READER MAGAZINE

CHRISTMAS GIFT OFFER!

Subscribers, do you know we offer a personal shopping service? Buy any subscription to *The Reader* and get **A FREE ONE-YEAR SUBSCRIPTION** for a friend! If we receive your instructions by 10th December, 2010, we will gift-wrap their first issue, add a personal message to a gift tag, and post it out to them in good time for the holidays. Simply include their name, address and your short message and leave the rest to us.

SUBSCRIPTION DISCOUNTS

Pay via annual Direct Debit and enjoy our lowest subscription price of just £18 per year. You can print off a form from our website, or call us on 0151 794 2830, or email leekeating@thereader.org.uk and we will send you a form in the post.

You can still save more than 30% on the recommended retail price of the magazine by taking out a 2- or 3-year subscription via cheque or PayPal. All prices include postage.

UK (p&p free)		
1 year	4 issues	£24.00
2 years	8 issues	£38.00
3 years	12 issues	£57.00

Abroad (p&p free)		
1 year	4 issues	£36.00
2 years	8 issues	£57.00
3 years	12 issues	£86.00

Please make cheques payable to The Reader Organisation and post to: The Reader Organisation, FREEPOST RSCJ-UHEY-XHXX, 19 Abercromby Square, L69 7ZG. Don't forget to include your name and address, and the issue number with which you would like your subscription to begin.

Overseas readers: the easiest way to take out a subscription is by using Paypal on our website: www.thereader.org.uk.

ESSAY

THE GREAT GAME

Michael Schmidt

The first English language recipient of the Nobel Prize in Literature (1907) Joseph Rudyard Kipling (1865–1936) was born in Bombay in 1865. His parents had courted in Staffordshire, walking beside the reservoir Lake Rudyard, and named their first-born for that long, narrow body of romantic water. His father, a professor of architectural sculpture (and later principal) at the Bombay school of art, became Principal of the School of Arts and curator of the Lahore Museum, Kim's 'Treasure House'. His mother was sister of Lady Burne-Jones and of Stanley Baldwin's mother. He did not come from the prosperous branch of the family but had considerable culture and influence at his disposal.

India in his early years was sufficient and wholly real to him. He felt at home there and it provided the foundation of his imagination and memory. He was under the care of Indian servants and spoke Hindustani better than English. This was more than a 'below stairs' experience of the Raj. Kim is the boy he would like to have been, the boy he imag-

MICHAEL SCHMIDT

ined being. When he was packed off to England as a little sahib, India became a lost world. He could revisit but never quite re-enter it. Much of his best writing is invested in reclaiming it for himself and others, children and adults.

He necessarily stood at an awkward angle to the Colonial world; the country he came to lacked the warmth, colour and easy intimacy of the one he left. He was 'only six', but by that age the deepest layers of imagination are already laid. He went from the warmth and active affection of his family home to live with an elderly evangelical relation in Southsea. The miserable time he spent there was relieved by occasional visits to the Burne-Jones establishment near Brighton. 'The circumstances of his early childhood in fact were uniquely valuable in his growth as a writer,' Kingsley Amis declares; 'without them, he would have been not only different but diminished.'

From the unhappiness of this life he passed at the age of fourteen to the United Services College at Westward Ho! (the one town in Britain with an exclamation mark in its name, the name itself a tribute to Charles Kingsley's novel), in Devonshire, a minor public school. There he began writing verses. *Schoolboy Lyrics* was printed privately when he was sixteen. The following year he returned to India to serve on the staff of the *Lahore Civil and Military Gazette*, contributing articles and verse.

E. Kay Robinson knew him at this time as 'a short, square, dark youth', bespectacled, and with 'an unlucky eye for colour [...] He had a weakness apparently for brown cloth with just that suggestion of ruddiness or purple in it which makes some browns so curiously conspicuous.' No matter: 'The charm of his manner [...] made you forget what he looked like in half a minute...' He had a habit of frequently rubbing his spectacles because 'he was always laughing; and when you laugh till you nearly cry your spectacles get misty. Kipling, shaking all over with laughter, and wiping his spectacles at the same time with his handkerchief'. He liked to invent pseudonyms, among them Esau Mull and Jacob Cavendish, and to indulge in parodies of his elders: 'Come under the Punkah, Maud.'

Kipling spent time with soldiers to find out how they think. Robinson again: 'He watched them at work and at play and at prayer from the points of view of all his confidants – the combatant officer, the doctor, the chaplain, the drill sergeant, and the private himself.' His approach was to learn first-hand, as a journalist does; journalism was his chief vocation, practised in India, in the South Africa of the Boer War, in the Far East, America and England. In relation to his Indian stories and to *Kim*, he saw deep into 'the strangely mixed manners of life and thought of the natives of India. He knew them all through their horizontal divisions of rank and their vertical sections of caste; their ramifications of race and blood; their antagonisms and blendings of creed; their heredi-tary strains of calling or handicraft.' He knew their languages, gestures and habits, quickly inspiring confidence so that even religious figures opened up to him. 'In two minutes the man – perhaps a wild hawk from the Afghan hills – would be pouring out into the ear of this sahib, with heaven-sent knowledge and sympathy, the weird tale of the blood feud and litigation, the border fray, and the usurer's iniquity, which had driven him so far afield'. It is difficult for the non-specialist to have an opinion about the precise accuracy of his portrayals, but there can be no doubt of their consistency or fictional coherence. Kim is his surrogate.

In 1887 he became foreign correspondent for the Allahabad *Pioneer* and began his travels. The sense that Kipling is a writer with inside in-formation is due to this journalistic training. So too are his sense of detail and a generally public tone that carries into his fiction. By the time he arrived in London in 1889, after a terminal row with the *Pioneer*, he had a reputation for his verse and prose. *The Story of the Gadsbys*, *Plain Tales from the Hills* and *The Phantom Rickshaw and other Eerie Tales* all appeared the year before, and *Departmental Ditties* (1886) had found its way to England as well. He had extensive introductions, met with and was fêted by writers, artists and political figures. Early popularity did not earn him the distrust of fellow writers. It was not then considered *de trop* for him to fix his eye on an audience. He developed his demotic Cockney dialect, experimental forms, and in his verse mastered traditional metrics in long and short measures as no poet since except for Auden has done. Henry James writes, with reserved approbation: 'No element assuredly in the artistic temperament of Mr Rudyard Kipling but operates with the ease and exactitude of an alarum clock set to the hour.'

By 1895 his reputation as a poet was so high that he may have been offered the poet laureateship in the wake of Tennyson, one of several honours he rejected. In later years he turned down the Order of Merit,

"The completeness of his experiences gave him a kind of apartness, even when he seems to speak familiarly."

and when his remains finally came to rest in Westminster Abbey in 1936, he was plain Rudyard Kipling. The completeness of his experi-ences – of the Raj, of the Empire for which he was apologist and elegist, of England, of the United States – gave him a kind of apartness, even when he seems to speak familiarly. This contributes to the impersonal-ity of his writing, a reluctance to dwell on subjective experience, a preference for hard completeness and a tone of truth-telling.

His politics, if they did not change, intensified in response to his experiences. The unsuccessful American experiment contributed to a hostility to America that appears in some productions; a strain of misogyny follows the failure of his marriage (like Stevenson, Kipling had trouble creating female characters); a constant sense of the mission of the Empire, and of Britain's falling short, rouses his greatest vehemence. He was not the conventional reactionary, a successful man growing old and wanting the world to stabilise and time to slow. For him there was urgency in arguing the case for the Empire even in its decline. He had seen it, had understood its cultures and potential, and he foresaw the consequences of its failure for Britain in the world. His reports, for instance during the Boer War, are brilliant because he was a fine correspondent, presenting surface events while understanding underlying causes. His *Letters of Travel* (1920) are full of fact and form.

But when in 1902 he retired, still a young man, to the ancient house of Bateman's in Burwash, Sussex and called it home for his remaining thirty-four years, his sense of himself in the world, and of England, changed. Amis regards the move to Bateman's as fatal: all of the best work, he affirms, was composed before that dark, low-browed house cast its enervating enchantment over him and Carrie. In this manorial

"It is hard not to feel, when reading Kipling's verse alongside his prose, that there is too much language in much of the verse."

retirement, beyond the fray, he was increasingly alone with his disappointments. Duty, sacrifice and devotion, his recurrent themes, were elicited particularly by the First World War, in which his only son was killed at the Battle of Loos. Hatred was one of the negative emotions that fed into his stories (less into the novels), and he was frank about it. Somerset Maugham was his not ungrateful beneficiary in this respect, speaking of 'Old Kipling, whom everyone despises so much these days', and wrote a valuable introduction to a selection of Kipling's fiction.

T.S. Eliot calls Kipling, at the outset, a ballad maker: we do not defend his poems against charges of obscurity but of 'excessive lucidity', and those who 'are exasperated by poetry which they do not understand' are also 'contemptuous of poetry which they understand without effort'. The fiction escapes this charge. It is hard not to feel, when reading Kipling's verse alongside his prose, that there is too much language in much of the verse. The prose is less profligate of means and effects. If Kipling is a poet of ideas, those ideas are already formed in his mind before the poem begins. Where the fiction is often an essay in discovery, the poems are expositions and iterations. Both at certain points insist on racial superiority, 'the Blood' that binds (specifically) the English, and a paternalism reserved for the people of the colonies grates.

But Kipling also wrote *Kim*. '*Kim* I must have read many times as child and man,' writes the poet Peter Scupham: 'a book whose embracing sympathies become richer with each successive reading as Kim

> *"Kim is a boy's book that becomes a book for grownups as well."*

himself changes from my childhood image of an alter-ego adventurer to my adult sense of him as a lodestone for many kinds of love.' This is a boy's book that becomes, like many novels of the period, a book for grownups as well. Scupham notes the 'manylayered tolerance and understanding in *Kim* – not always associated with Kipling'. Critics construct his politics selectively to find a crude consistency that some work flatly contradicts. Kipling is not a consistent racist, sadist, protofascist or feudalist, terms critics have applied to him. As novelist he is neither philosopher nor ideologue. He claims the freedom to start a new book, find a new path or reopen an old one.

Kim was published in 1901. Kimball O'Hara lives his picaresque life begging and running dubious missions in a Lahore based closely upon the city Kipling knew. Kim is an orphan, his late father a dissolute Irish soldier, his mother also perished. Various natives, ignorant of his identity, patronise him, notable among them Mahbub Ali, a Pashtun or Afghan involved in the Great Game between two empires vying for influence in the sub-continent, the British and the Russian, and trading horses across borders. Hence he is familiar with great swathes of India and is free to move about. The book begins with the meeting between Kim and the man who becomes his master and his responsibility, an unworldly Tibetan Lama seeking the mysterious River of the Arrow to wash himself clean and transcend the Wheel of Things. They take one another under their wings; Kim becomes his *chela* or disciple without forfeiting his worldly cunning. Protecting and leading his master, the boy experiences all the peoples and places of India and comes to understand how the British systems of control and repression work. He is drawn into the secret service, tested and proven, his coming of age a various and exciting process. Though it becomes known that he is English, he is never reduced but, like Mowgli in the *Jungle Book*, preserves his uniqueness and lives between the many worlds that are India and the other world of Britain and its Empire. The characters he encounters are defined by speech, costume and the place they occupy in the hierarchy. Kim is credibly at home in their languages and cultures. The events that take place in Simla, where he encounters Lurgan Sahib and learns about gem stones, are among the most vivid. It was at Simla that Kipling spent his vacations from the heat of summer: 'pure joy – every golden hour counted. It began in heat and discomfort, by rail and road. It ended in the cool evening, with a wood fire in one's bedroom, and next morn – thirty more of them ahead! – the early cup of tea, the Mother who brought it in, and the long talks of us all together again.'

In the Simla scenes in *Kim* the protagonist discovers his true karma. As Lurgan Sahib performs incomprehensible magic with the gem-stones Kim – to retain his courage – makes a decisive shift and we know he is changing form: 'So far Kim had been thinking in Hindi, but a tremor came on him, and with an effort like that of a swimmer before sharks, who hurls himself half out of the water, his mind leaped up from a darkness that was swallowing it and took refuge in – the multiplication-table in English!' That exclamation mark expresses the narrator's own surprise at his protagonist's instinctive defences. When his education is complete, Kim's Lama would let him go, but Kim wants to stay with this man who is his spirit's beloved and his father. 'I am not a Sahib. I am thy *chela*,' he insists. But the boy who was the Friend of All the World is becoming a young Englishman.

When in 1889 Kipling left India for a second time, having lost his job, he travelled east, to Burma, China, Japan, and then to San Francisco. He wrote sketches and articles for *The Pioneer*. Unlike most British travellers to the United States, Kipling arrived on the West Coast, then travelled north to Canada, exploring the continental American West and the frontier, befriending Mark Twain when he finally reached Elmira, New York. In the autumn he arrived in England once more, travelled down to London, and found himself already known as a writer. A plaque in Villiers Street, above a sherry wine importer and a pleasant wine bar, marks where he lived and conceived some of his books. Here he completed his first novel, *The Light that Failed*, about a painter who loses his sight and meets a particularly melodramatic Kiplingesque death – in battle. 'His luck had held to the last, even to the crowning mercy of a kindly bullet through his head.' There is a paragraph break in which we wipe our eyes. 'Torpenhow knelt under the lee of the camel, with Dick's body in his arms.' *Finis* in both senses.

This intense, uneven novel was followed by a nervous breakdown, and then a close friendship with the American Wolcott Balestier, a book agent who collaborated with Kipling on another novel. In the interests of his mental health, he resumed his travels. In India, on learning of Balestier's early death, he hurried back to England, having proposed marriage to Balestier's sister Carrie by telegram. She accepted by the same medium, a succinct exchange. They married in early 1892 and their life together started rosily enough; they travelled widely and then, after financial reversals, settled in Brattleboro, Vermont, near Carrie's family, renting a little house, Bliss Cottage, and setting it to rights. Their first child was born there and Kipling wrote some of his best work, including the *Jungle Books*, indebted for its inspiration in part to Rider Haggard's *Nada the Lily*. The Kiplings built their own house and he wrote there a favourite book of many boys of my generation, *Captains Courageous* (1897), in which a spoilt brat falls overboard from his father's yacht and is picked up by a fishing boat and subjected to manly discipline, finding his true nature once the veneer of affectation and indulgence has been harshly sanded away. This story too ends in melodrama and we realise that the superiority of *Kim* is in its understatement and open-endedness. But in the sea writing of *Captains Courageous* there are touches worthy of Maryatt and early Melville. Life in Vermont ended, after a messy family quarrel. In 1896 he left the United States for good.

It is conventional to present Kipling's later years as grim, fluctuating between anger and resignation, his politics a mess of prejudice. After the decline of his marriage and his son's death, his anger with the Establishment of which he was such a formidable representative burst out in ways that alarmed his friends. But his later years were not uniformly sour. Success is a tonic, even for the lonely heart. Hugh Walpole remembers the sixty-one year old Kipling at the Athenaeum, sitting amongst the reviews of his most recent book, 'beaming like a baby'. It is possible to exaggerate his isolation and disappointment. He still wrote, and could write well, even if he did not think as much or as analytically as he had done, even though he could no longer read the runes with the clarity he had in the days of his investigative travels. Was H.G. Wells satirising Kipling in that chapter of *The Island of Dr Moreau* in which 'the Beast-Men are seen mumbling their pathetic Laws', since the actual rhetoric of the *Jungle Book* had become rooted in the popular mind along with many of the poems, 'If –' in particular. Pritchett puts Wells and Kipling together. They are 'obviously divergent branches of the same tree. Wells the Utopian, Kipling the patriot – they represent the day-dreams of the lower middle class which will either turn to socialism or fascism.' This is the same dialectical irresolution that marks the British imagination in the 1930s and again in the 1970s. 'Opposed in tendency, Wells and Kipling both have the vision of artists; they foresee the conditions of our time. They both foretold the violence with a certain appetite.'

Kipling lost some popularity when he began to stigmatise his core readership by insisting on the hard truths underlying his – and their – ideology. Jingoism had fed on his writing, his verse in particular, providing it with anthems. At the Victory ceremony after the Boer War ended, outside the Transvaal Parliament 10,000 soldiers gave voice to 'Recessional'. The apparently wholesome 'what oft was thought' of his verse and prose gave way, in some later works, to 'what was never flushed out into the open before'. 'The Islanders' was a poisoned chalice for his political admirers: Angus Wilson describes how it 'takes each

"Kipling was read, even during the decades when it was not pukka to read him."

sacred cow of the clubs and senior common rooms and slaughters it messily before its worshippers' eyes'. J.M. Barrie acidly declared, 'Mr. Kipling has yet to learn that a man may know more of life staying at home by his mother's knee than swaggering in bad company over three continents.' Barrie was a 'mother's knee' man who kept charming company. H.L. Mencken chides 'those brummagem emotion-squeezers of the Kipling type' when he describes what Conrad was up against: 'their playhouse fustian and their naive ethical cocksureness'.

But Kipling is still read, even during the decades when it was not pukka to read him. The Definitive Edition of his works had gone through sixty impressions by 1982. Unit sales of the most popular of his books were and remain substantial. One of his paradoxical achievements Richard Le Gallienne dwells on: he regained for the poet 'some of that serious respect from his fellow-citizens which, under a misapprehension of his effeminacy and general uselessness, he had lost awhile'. The 'his' here refers to Oscar Wilde's notoriety. Kipling restores manly respect for a vocation Wilde had discredited. 'The poet is not so much a joke to the multitude as he was a few years ago…' This little, lonely man is caricatured by Max Beerbohm in his Savile Club cartoon as dwarfish, his thinning hair combed flat on his outsized skull, aggressively attentive to a debate: an unlikely redeemer of British masculinity (the Nobel Prize citation praised his 'virility of ideas'), and physically an implausible champion of the imperial ideal. In the same cartoon a pointy-faced Thomas Hardy looks on, unamused, and there is Gosse, too, and other players in that parallel Great Game, the *fin-de-siècle* literary comedy.

This essay is from a draft of *Lives of the Novelists*, a huge undertaking which Michael Schmidt is working on at present.

POETRY

LINDA CHASE

Mittens

From where I parked my car, green mittens on new snow
must have been visible from the only house across the road.
Inside, a family sat down to eat. I could see them.

Was it the moon, or just because the dog began to bark?
Was it because the snow had finally finished falling,
or because the mother watched the dog who watched the road?

In someone's eye a bit of green lodged like tangled wool,
eventually needing her attention. 'The Aga will be on all night,'
she may have thought as she pulled on her boots and gloves.

This is what I know: I lost my mittens. I found my mittens,
dry inside a plastic bag hanging from the aerial of my car.
It wasn't snowing any more. It was simply crisp and even.

Sotto Voce

In her quiet times she let
all conversation pass and yet
she also felt the urge to speak
but could not. Thoughts were dumb, oblique,
distorted, slipping from her mind
as if chaos had been designed
by mutes, who smothered every sound.
'Don't speak.' Suffocated, bound,
her voice was choked, her words were drowned,
her thoughts confused, though once profound
were stifled in her throat, her mouth
her teeth, her tongue her balking breath.
Quiet, blurred, her ideas swirled
around her silent inner world
until a sentence came to her,
complete with subject and a verb
no adjectives, no adverb clutter,
it came, went, a muffled mutter
hardly heard, then faded straight away.
 'I speak,' was all she had to say.

YOUR REGULARS

A PIECE AND TWO PREAMBLES

Ian McMillan

Ｐeople have been looking at me lately and saying one of two things; either 'You look well' or 'Have you had your hair cut?' The subtext of this (as literary critics say) is that I'm presenting a different face to the world. The fact is, I've lost weight. I've lost loads of weight through abandoning pies and beer, and every morning I do a few geriatric exercises and then go for a walk down Snape Hill and back up Upperwood Road as fast as I can without breaking into a run. And because the sight of somebody power walking in Barnsley is unusual, I clutch a letter as I walk so that people think I'm going to the post box.

And the point of this preamble is that I meant to get fit when I hit forty, but I actually didn't start losing weight and doing the exercise until I got beyond fifty. The fact is, there are certain things you should do before you're forty, certain books you should read, certain authors you should discover, and perhaps certain kinds of book you should leave behind forever. If you leave it till you're fifty it might be almost too late, and you'll end up power walking up a suburban street with an envelope in your hand rather than running a double marathon.

So, when I got to forty I determined that I would read, as well as watch, Shakespeare. I told myself that I would read all his plays, starting at the front of the volume of Collected Plays I'd had since I was a sixth-former when my Auntie bought it for me 'to improve myself'. The book was in more or less chronological order, so I started with *Henry VI*, parts one, two and three and progressed from there via *Richard III* and *The Comedy of Errors* to *Titus Andronicus*, where I kind of got stuck. Maybe I was approaching it in the wrong way, in a new-year's-resolution spirit of dashing at something far too quickly, embracing it far too tightly. I determined that I'd read a set amount (five pages, as I seem to remember) every night before I went to bed, like I was saying my prayers or learning my Latin verbs.

And maybe that was the problem: I wasn't reading the whole thing, getting a sense of the sweep of the narrative or the epic nature of the action. I was just nibbling away at it, not having time to develop an understanding of the characters or the plot, I was just casting my eyes, rather than my mind, over a certain wordage every twenty-four hours as though I was building a wall. And so, by the time I was 40 and a half, I stopped reading them. I tried again with Dickens; again, same bull-in-a-china-shop approach, same initial determination, same tailing off to the listless flicking of pages until I couldn't remember what I'd read. After Dickens (and I would now be the grand old age of 41. Even 42!) I gave up my completist project and stuck to just reading books as they came up, because I'd heard about the author, or the first two pages intrigued me as I read them in a bookshop or I'd read a good review or I just liked the cover.

And the point of this second preamble is that I've just been on Desert Island Discs, and along with my records (they weren't that keen on Captain Beefheart but they loved Vaughan Williams) I had to choose a book to take with me and when I was making my list of suggestions I wished that, all those years before, I'd carried on with my Dickens reading and carried it on to other authors, maybe concentrating on Nobel Prize in Literature Winners or translated writers or writers whose name began with a random letter of the alphabet pulled from a hat because then I'd know much more about the grand sweep of literature than I do.

I wasn't so bothered about not finishing the Shakespeare, because as far as I can recall, you still get to take that with you to the island. Part of the problem of choosing the book for the show is that you don't want to appear silly in front of Kirsty or in front of the millions of listeners. At college I tried to impress a girl from Walsall by telling her that I was a big fan of Goethe. Except I pronounced it Go-eth, and there's always that possibility of humiliation when you're trying to pick the book you'll take to the island with you.

At first I thought I might take a big fat novel but then I decided that, for better or worse, I can take my time with poetry much more than I can with prose. With a novel, naturally, I make my way from the beginning to the end. With poetry I can wallow or dip, I can turn the pages backwards to remind me where I've been and flick ahead to give me a hint of where I might be going. I wanted to take something difficult but inspiring, something I knew I could read as the seasons changed and the calendar turned. I thought of the inexhaustible John Ashbery, or the sometimes unfathomable Tom Raworth. I almost selected a nature writer, like Harriet Tarlo or Peter Larkin, and I was very tempted by the great Gael Turnbull.

In the end, though, I plumped for *The Long and The Short of It*, the collected poems of the great Roy Fisher, published by Bloodaxe. There's humour there, and difficulty, and compassion and artistry and I know that, because I've been reading Roy Fisher since well before I turned forty, that he'll be a marvellous companion for me as the coconuts ripen and fall...

REVIEWS

'NOW I AM GROWN UP'
THE WRITING OF ELIZABETH TAYLOR

Tessa Hadley

N. H. Reeve, *Elizabeth Taylor*
Northcote/British Council: Tavistock, 2008
ISBN 978-0-7463-1155-4

The work of reading is partly a continuous reassessment; time passes and books, reshuffled, fall into new places in our taste and in our history. Certain writers of the mid-twentieth century may have seemed old-fashioned even in their own time; when Robbe-Grillet and Sartre held the field, where to place Elizabeth Taylor, lady-ex-librarian in High Wycombe, wife of a confectioner, mother of two? She sounds herself like the kind of old-fashioned novel she might have written. (And if putting High Wycombe alongside Sartre seems heavy-handed, then here's a contemporary review of Taylor's *A Wreath of Roses* in the *New Statesman*, 1949: 'Virtually no "thinking" in the intellectual sense at all … Besides the rays of [Sartre's] powerful and adventurous mind… Miss Elizabeth Taylor's country cottages and pubs, her artists, discontented wives, and mysterious strangers, seem to dissolve and melt away into transparency'.[1]) In the decades after Taylor's death in 1975, her books naturally sank in that trough of irrelevance where most books sink when they're fatally recent but not new enough, before re-emerging into literary history proper. (Of course certain readers – and publishers: good for Virago – kept faith through that purgatorial time.)

From our perspective fifty, sixty years later, the whole picture of the literature of that period starts to have a different shape. Some of the grandest narratives written then turn out to read tediously, and some of the parish histories seem, out of their very limitations, to open up onto the largest perspectives.[2] (Some of the grand narratives turn out to be parish histories.) As the realities of 'country cottages and pubs…artists, discontented wives' are lost to us, at least in the form that Taylor knew them, her pictures of suburban and domestic life take on new potency. Her world is made strange as history leaves it beached behind us; we're not so inclined to condescend to it. The fictions' survival, now, will depend upon the precision and force with which the writing's lens, then, was bent upon its subject. At the level of the sentence, the *aperçu*, the captured texture of a moment, if a writer can make us freshly surprised by what no longer exists, then the books will carry their stories and their point into a different age.

Behind the surface of Taylor's quiet life there were surprises: the Communist Party (her biographer records a story that she may have washed the feet of the Jarrow marchers!), and a couple of love affairs (one before her marriage, one, lasting and tormented, after it). Nonetheless, her story demonstrates reassuringly how a writing life (twelve novels, four collections of stories) can grow out of next to nothing – or just out of books. She did it all by herself – as soon as she left school, almost before she was adult, she made up her mind that she wanted to be a novelist, and began to try; there was no library at home to encourage her, no clever set of writers in the family, no university degree – though there was amateur dramatics. 'She seemed instinctively to know she would be a writer', says Don Potter (a woodcarver in Gill's circle, and her first lover). There's a wonderful letter written in 1942, to Ray Russell[3] in a POW camp in Austria (her first story would be published in 1944, her first novel, *At Mrs Lippincote's*, in 1945):

One day I will write well. I have not done so up till now. I have written very badly and sentimentally, with only here and there the seeds of reality scattered among the falsity of the whole. I wrote before because I wanted to get things straight. Well, that's understandable. It may be necessary as a means of finding one's way. Now I am grown up. I took a long time doing it. My childhood went on too long. But now I begin to understand.

Taylor's signature style is there in the sentences of the letter – unornamented, precise, crisply analytic, rather staccato, merciless. 'Style,' she wrote, 'is personality and the seat of love.'[4] Here she is in her 1953 novella, *Hester Lilly*: Hester Lilly, orphaned, has come to live with her much older cousin Robert, working for him as a secretary. He is headmaster at a boys' school; inevitably she falls in love with him, and when she weeps in his study, cautiously he decides not to comfort her. 'Twice before he had taken her in his arms, on two of the three times they had been together. He had met her when she came home from Singapore where her father had died, and she had begun to cry in the station refreshment room where they were having a cup-of-tea. His earlier meeting was at her christening when he had dutifully, as godfather, nursed her for a moment.' Neil Reeve says that Taylor's style has 'an air of practical competence about it, of knowing how to do things and use things, without fuss or display... nothing escaping notice or being beneath notice' (p.5). On the one hand, perception is made out of the narration of solidities – facts and times and things that happened, conjured through concrete detail (the station refreshment room, the cup-of-tea, a man dutifully nursing a bundle of shawls). On the other hand, the concrete details aren't left to work by themselves, impressionistically; there's always commentary, luminous with intelligence, weaving them together: '... as he stood at the window, listening to her tears, he knew that she was collapsed, abandoned, ready for his embrace of consolation, and he would not turn around, though his instinct was to go to her'.

The commentary imagines empathetically, and with intensity, naming emotions; then makes a characteristically comic move. 'Without physical contact he could not see how to bring the scene to an end. Bored, he surveyed the garden and thought that the box hedge needed trimming.' (Chekhov's Gurov, in *Lady with a Lapdog*, is bored while his new love waxes emotional, and cuts a slice of melon – his prose seems to make just this same move.) The precise solidity of that box hedge is essential; comedy and intensity tug at one another, anchoring the material in a position that's neither light nor earnest but holds both possibilities in ironic tension. Presumably that poise is what Taylor struggled to achieve, through the apprentice novels she wrote and then destroyed in her twenties (though she was also struggling all that wartime, and through the period of her membership of the CP, with 'relevance' – 'you write because you must, not because it would be a useful thing to do, & this effort to direct it into useful channels has been death to my writing in the last seven years... I am simply hustling back into the ivory tower & moan for the wasted years & the delusions I had. What utter cock it all was.')

The little worlds of Taylor's novels and stories – declining seaside resort, boarding school, small town, hotel – aren't ever safe havens, or pockets of nostalgic Englishness (anyway, she writes about London too). There's something in her sensibility too scorching and penetrating to come comfortably to rest anywhere. The boarding school in *Hester Lilly* isn't timeless – Hester Lilly is befriended by a drunk old woman in the village whose family once owned the house that's now the school ('Our home since the Dark Ages. Three houses, at least, on this site and brasses in the church going back to the Crusades. Now there are only the graves left'). *A Wreath of Roses* (1949) opens with passengers waiting in what could be a charmingly sleepy country station, for a train that doesn't come; on page three, however, a stranger kills himself, jumping from a footbridge in front of the express (he falls wide, but dies anyway). Unsettling enough; but at least in any more conventional novel-world, that disaster ought at least to precipitate the plot. Here, it only serves as a sort of annunciatory chord for the story to come, the intrusion of a sinisterly blank con-man into a friendship between three women: he pretends to be an ex-soldier, returning emotionally damaged from the war. 'A peculiarly *noir* concatenation,' Reeve calls it, 'of real feelings and false ones, cynicism, self deception...'

These novels do work in terms of a realist literary tradition; we're meant to be transported across the books' thresholds into their worlds, and the writing strives to create the illusion of actual time passing, plausible causation, and so on. But they're hardly impervious to modernism; on the contrary, close behind their narrow focus and their almost stagy concentration on a few lives locked together, the quirky influence of Ivy Compton Burnett, among others, is unmistakeable. For that matter, there's even something of Beckett, whose *Happy Days* Taylor identified with strongly: 'Really devastating, and as much as one can bear – a middle-aged woman's gallantry'. (She went to see it with Ivy, who was more interested in the chocolates than the play). Yet somehow Compton Burnett went on 'counting', well into the seventies, as innovative and experimental, at the same time that some readers were finding Taylor too suggestive of 'the tinkle of tea-cups'.[5]

Reeve writes very well about the complex cultural positioning of certain women writers – Bowen, Rose Macaulay, Rebecca West, Rosamond Lehmann, and Taylor herself – in the mid-twentieth century. They were often relegated by critics, he says, to a '"no-man's land" between the "highbrow" and the "middlebrow"'. 'Their work has obvious density and intelligence, and often poses severe imaginative challenges; but because so much of their material was drawn from the conventions of romantic or domestic fiction, and from the aspirations and anxieties of their predominantly middle-class readership, these writers tended to be regarded as insufficiently searching and innovative to be numbered unequivocally among the modernist élite.' (p.2) The markers for distinguishing 'serious' or 'highbrow' fiction are themselves not always pure, but subject to fashion. 'Modernism', which saw itself as objectively diagnostic of society, while 'realism' simply represented the symptoms, was – we see from our vantage point now – itself part of a machinery of cultural (and gendered) hierarchy.

The dividing line, anyway, where realism meets experiment in fiction, is never so clear cut. It is true that in Taylor's writing, attention is not drawn explicitly, or formally (as in *Ulysses*, say), to the artifice sustaining the illusion. Her novels and stories rest at ease inside conventions of structure and suggestion built over a couple of centuries – so well-established they can be deployed with the merest indication, the lightest touch. Yet a certain deliberate stylishness, a 'manner', is surely also meant to draw attention to the fiction at work on the page, between the reader and the dream. In the following couple of sentences of description, for instance, taken almost at random from *A Wreath of Roses*, the incantatory rhythm and the repetition ('cow') do something else as well as try to capture a posited 'real' moment. They also *enjoy themselves*. 'And now (the landscape opening always like a succession of fans) cows moved deep in buttercups, hedges were dense and creamy with elderflower and cow-parsley. Yet her pleasure in it all was ruined…' (p.11) The complex management of voice and breath required to read that rightly, feel distinctive in the delivery as brushstrokes in a painting. That odd image of the fans, hallucinatory if you visualise it strictly (is that how landscapes replace one another rapidly beyond a train window – like fans opening?), suggests how landscape can seem painted, artificial, on the glass of the train window – or in the words of a novel, printed on a page while mining the recesses of our inner store of pictures.

Also, Taylor's prose seems to acknowledge itself precisely as belonging at its attenuated long distance away from the fresh beginnings of the realist novel tradition. Isn't there something deliberately and defiantly old-fashioned, sometimes, in the work and in the language? Her writing (and some of the rest of the best women's writing of the mid-century) doesn't so much take for granted certain well-established fictional expectations (and certain subjects, and certain types – 'artists, discontented wives, mysterious strangers'), as relish re-entering, late, these old shapes worn so smooth under other hands. The finished surface of her subjects is something like the high gloss of a treatment worked over and over, differently each time.

Reeve thinks that there's a distinctive Taylor late style (and he makes explicitly the connection with Beckett, too).

…as Taylor's work becomes more preoccupied with ageing, with narrowing prospects – in *The Wedding Group*, even most of the younger characters seem prematurely old – new things happen to her style. The voice directing the novels is increasingly dry and laconic; sentences and paragraphs are pared right down, producing an extraordinary compressed vitality of narrative comment, with so much simmering under so much composure. (p.67)

Her last novel, *Blaming* (1976), 'simmers' deliciously. Taylor wrote it when she was already ill with the cancer which would kill her at 63; it's a tough, funny and bleakish book, about a flawed friendship between two ill-matched women. Amy is savage with anger because she's newly widowed, and Martha is a helpful American who demands more house-room in return for her kindness than Amy is able to yield up. ('Mourning seemed to give the go-ahead to every sort of rudeness and selfishness', Amy's son thinks, p. 36). Its pared-down characterisation and scene-setting, its whiff of brutality and its minimally delicate visuals (there's an extraordinary hotel room where Amy sits grieving in Istanbul, in the hours after her husband's death – draped with dark red, 'a huge, muslin covered bed with a chandelier above it and a velvet armchair'): these constitute the perfect restricted palette for this sideways-on, narrowly focused study of the bourgeois-arty sixties and seventies in England. Old forms of life (Amy's riverside house with its view of mud flats, seedy manservant, William Morris wallpaper) muddle up against new ones (cheap foreign holidays, Martha's sexual disinhibition, and her frank and humourless writing, which Amy can't bring herself to like). The novel isn't inclined to indulge in either direction. Amy's grumpy hostility – for instance – to her daughter-in-law (too busy with family-planning clinics, pollution, prisons, marriage guidance), is given the same coolly comic treatment as her son's impatience with his mother's gracelessness. All these relationships are lacking, they all ought to love one another better. Yet the writing never gathers any head of steam behind its 'blaming'. The moral space in the novel is certainly uneasy (its finale, with Martha's suicide, is dramatically sad); it's also roomy, elastic and forgiving.

Amy dreads looking after her granddaughters Dora and Isobel ('"She always sleeps like this and wakes up in a temper and screams all the time she's getting dressed," [Dora] promised Amy'), but despite all her efforts is roped in from time to time to help. The portrait of the two girls is a vein of rich excess in a book about life drawn painfully thin: warm, exactly observed, unsentimental. Here, for example, one of the girls has had treats and is gloating to the other. The little girls don't do anything so simplifying to the novel as redeem it – but they do gor-geously embody appetite, curiosity, the future.

> **Dora was sitting at the kitchen table, drawing, and she went on drawing against the spate of Isobel's descriptions of taxis, ice-creams, Americans and Christmas decorations. Trying not to listen, she frowned and pursed her lips. At last she said calmly, scribbling pubic hair into her drawing of a nude woman, "I've decided when I've grown up I'm going to be a great artist like Grandpa."**
>
> **"I'm going to be a great artist too," Isobel said. "I shall make someone do the drawings, and I shall colour them in."**

Neil Reeve has written a very good book about Taylor's work – good in its placing of her work in a critical and literary-historical context, and particularly good in its finely and minutely intelligent readings of the books' detail. Fittingly, given Taylor's own history with the critics, this is a kind of criticism that came for a while to look 'old-fashioned', but which – in the general collapse of enchantment with the scientific and philosophical treatments of literature – should be coming round again for recognition. Louder kinds of criticism drown out the particularity of the individual writer's voice and subject-world, enlisting their works for generalisation; this critical book sets about catching a writer's distinctiveness and characterising it.

...the instant capture of different kinds of self-absorption; the comic, desolate distances between those apparently close; the commanding poise of the narrative voice, opening horizons around the moment over which the reader could brood almost endlessly. (p.1)

Although that summary sits at the head of the book, it's an indication of Reeve's approach that he uses, to embark on an opening generalisation, a specific passage from the work (in fact, from *Blaming*). This is criticism at the level of the sentence; text in hand, the critic makes connections, extrapolates from metaphor, interprets, makes explicit what's implicit in the original, draws out themes, makes connections to other texts within the *oeuvre* and outside it. Kermode in *The Sense of an Ending* writes that while poets 'help us to make sense of our lives', critics are only bound to attempt 'making sense of the ways we try to make sense of our lives'; the best criticism never aims to supplant or outshine its original. A study like Reeve's fills out the imperfections of our reading; dwells on the work with an intensity, and for a passage of time, commensurate with the intensity and time the novelist spent on writing it. Literature's best intricacy and precision work half-subliminally, reading at normal speed: Reeve opens up these riches, and the serious implications of this writer's art, for our discussion. There is room in the world for all kinds of critical responses, beginning with fiction as their starting point; 'brooding around the moment' is perhaps of all of them the most truly readerly.

1. Quoted in *The Other Elizabeth Taylor*, Nicola Beauman, Persephone Books: London 2009, p. 214. The review is by Julia Strachey.
2. I've borrowed 'parish histories' from political theorist John Dunn, who thinks, rightly I'm sure, that we need to go beyond them in politics. But fiction's different.
3. Beauman, p. 98. Ray Russell was the second lover. He was a worker at a fireboard mill in High Wycombe and a fellow CP member.
4. Reeve, p. 5. (It's from 'Novelists and their Novels', in *Vogue*, July 1951.)
5. This was Saul Bellow, Booker prize judge in 1971, when Taylor's *Mrs. Palfrey at the Clairmont* was shortlisted. Beauman, p. 369.

THE OLD POEM

MICHAEL DRAYTON (1563–1631)

'SINCE THERE'S NO HELP'

Sarah Coley

Since there's no help, come, let us kiss and part –
Nay, I have done: you get no more of me;
And I am glad, yea, glad with all my heart
That thus so cleanly I myself can free;
Shake hands forever, cancel all our vows,
And when we meet at any time again,
Be it not seen in either of our brows
That we one jot of former love retain.
Now at the last gasp of love's latest breath,
When, his pulse failing, passion speechless lies,
When faith is kneeling by his bed of death,
And innocence is closing up his eyes –
    Now if thou wouldst, when all have given him over,
    From death to life thou mightst him yet recover.

ON 'SINCE THERE'S NO HELP'

Though modern readers sometimes may react against old poetry – the perceived artifice of the diction and the formal perfection of the verse – Michael Drayton is unlikely to make you bridle for those reasons. Bluntly spoken and decisive, he sounds like a man's man from any age. I imagine him in denim and biker's boots. In the first eight lines of the sonnet, every phrase links to an action, pulling the reader into the real time of the poem: 'Since there's no help, come, let us kiss and part'. The lines are like stage directions and you can watch the fluctuations between the poet and the woman: 'Nay' – she feels remorse, or maybe she likes the kiss – 'Nay, I have done: you get no more of me'. He talks in absolutes with his eye on the future: 'I am glad, yea, glad with *all* my heart', 'Shake hands *forever*, cancel *all* our vows', as if at parting he took away the whole of himself uninjured and intact, 'glad… that thus so cleanly I myself can free'. But here's the first little tremor of doubt. That bold word 'free' links back to 'no help' in the first line – both are types of existence beyond the call of ordinary cares, one imposed, one chosen. The parting isn't chosen by him but he fights to transform helplessness into freedom.

The big change and turnaround happens with the last six lines, as often in the sonnet form. 'Now' he says, and suddenly all control breaks down. His confidence before was the confidence of imagination or will. 'Forever' seemed easy but 'Now' is unsupportably hard. The language starts to splinter and grow complex, 'Now at the last gasp of love's latest breath'. 'Last' grows out of 'latest' but is succeeded by it in the line, stretching the moment impossibly, as if beyond finality you would find a new timescale possible. The decisiveness of the first lines is replaced by this extended image of lingering death, and he's no longer directing affairs but lying helpless at the centre. It's almost invisible at first that he has said '*love*'s latest breath' – all of the time parting had no other language than that of love itself, no other context. Most significantly, you can feel the loss of control in the crowd of would-be helpers that appear around the man in his trouble, those facets of himself, 'love', 'passion', 'faith' and 'innocence'. The powers that would connect him back to life and stir him are dying there is nothing he can do. But then:

> Now if thou wouldst, when all have given him over,
> From death to life thou mightst him yet recover.

Her return to the poem is electrifying, drawing together in the present moment (still 'Now') both her independence and her power to transform everything, 'if thou wouldst'. It seems to me both a ravishing kind of love poem and almost like prayer in the man's dependence upon a help he cannot command.

READERS CONNECT
WITH
OXFORD WORLD'S CLASSICS

MARK TWAIN
PUDD'NHEAD WILSON AND OTHER TALES

Is it more of a novel, a fable or a folk tale? Like a folk tale it's a story of two children, one free, one slave, swapped over in infancy by Roxana, their nurse and mother and twins from Italy who bring art and magic to the stifling community of Dawson's Landing. Like fable it morally

Mark Twain
Pudd'nhead Wilson
and Other Tales

OXFORD WORLD'S CLASSICS

exposes the hypocrisy and idiocy of slavery, an inheritance we still live with whereby an apparently white woman, Roxana, is counted a slave because one-sixteenth of her is black with all the stereotypes invented by prejudice thrust upon her, just as the cleverest man in town becomes a 'puddinghead' because its inhabitants can't understand irony. But in the end, this is triumphantly a novel because the characters inhabit these confusions so that the clarities of fable become the densities of life. The villain, Tom, is accepted as 'white' though he is in fact 'black', and the criminality, meanness and cowardice ascribed to his racial mix derive actually from his over-indulged boyhood and his own character, as unique as the fingerprints that produce the resolution in what is also a detective story and a courtroom drama. The heart of the book in every sense is Roxana, his 'black' mother, raped by one of the town's 'gentlemen', a woman of courage and resource, yet half-willingly victimised by her worthless son. When she reveals to Tom his father's identity she remains trapped by the prejudices under which she suffers:

> She put on a little prouder air, if possible, and added impressively: 'Does you 'member Cunnel Cecil Burleigh Essex, dat died de same year yo' young Marse Tom Driscoll's pappy died, en all de Masons en Odd Fellers en Churches turned out en give him de bigges' funeral dis town ever seed? Dat's de man.'
>
> Under the inspiration of her soaring complacency the departed graces of her earlier days returned to her, and her bearing took to itself a dignity and state that might have passed for queenly if her surroundings had been a little more in keeping with it.

It's also bleakly funny.

Colin Gray is a retired English teacher starting a Read Aloud group in Hereford

For lovers of the unadulterated Twain voice such as myself, this is a disappointing story. It has the attributes of a greater book – Roxy and her son are characters of tragic potential and the scenes of small town life on the Mississippi are lively (especially the climactic trial scene), but I didn't find the probing of identity and character convincing: comic plot and moral theme don't fit easily together. All the same, the book has raw ingredients for a good screenplay.

* *

Lynne Hatwell (dovegreyreader) is a Devon-based community nurse

Having made good friends with Mark Twain after reading and loving *The Prince and the Pauper* as a child, the friendship had remained untested until *Pudd'nhead Wilson* arrived. Sadly this book has sorely tested our acquaintance. Despite some similarities in the plot (swapping places, nature versus nurture), there was nothing here to enjoy and it eventually became a rather confusing read. I'm afraid I surrendered before the end.

*

Mette Steenberg is the founder/director of Laeseforeningen, (The Reading Society) in Denmark

Pudd'nhead Wilson was a fun and instructive read, or rather listen as my audiobook spoke to me on the train in a heavy Southern accent. A tale of how wrong leads to more wrong and truth lasts the longest, enacted by characters who feel real enough for you to want to receive a lesson from them. I particularly enjoyed the chapter epigraphs from Wilson's calendar: 'Let us endeavour so to live that when we come to die even the undertaker will be sorry'.

* * *

Drummond Moir, once of Edinburgh, works for a London-based publisher

'A Nigger! I am a nigger! Oh, I wish I was dead!' cries the wretched Tom on discovering his true origins. If you enjoy novels that offer insight into past prejudices, the pervasive racism of *Pudd'nhead Wilson*, at once casual and ferocious, will be fascinating. But if you need more from a novel than half-baked characters and a bafflingly predictable plot, I'd steer clear of this oddly clumsy novel.

0

STAR RATINGS

***** one of the best books I've read   ** worth reading
**** one of the best I've read this year   * not for me but worth trying
*** highly recommended   0 don't bother

THE READING REVOLUTION

DIARIES OF THE READER ORGANISATION

Alexis McNay

There's a passage of dialogue in *The Road* by Cormac McCarthy where the boy seeks again the assurance from his father that there are others like them:

> **There are other good guys. You said so.**
> **Yes.**
> **So where are they?**
> **They're hiding.**
> **Who are they hiding from?**
> **From each other.**

We're reading this in Phoenix House rehabilitation centre, where nine or ten readers recovering from drug or alcohol dependency have huddled around this book weekly for about four months. The book, though beautiful, is demanding, sometimes harrowing, asking its characters to find reserves of humanity – even if that makes physical survival harder – because it's the only way to really survive. Yet, week to week, I look around at the returning faces, many of whom have been there since the start of the journey. Those that know the story relate it to the newcomers, as if describing people they know.

The rehab is a community brought together in a spirit of hope, but coming from a culture in which some deception – of others and of self – has been felt to be a necessity. There's ample good to be felt in the room, but some of it is guarded, some mistrusted. What's needed is an intermediary, and *The Road* provides it. Readers reveal themselves by talking outside of themselves. Later in the story, the man and the boy reach the coast and the ocean, such as it is. It's as bleak as everything they've passed through on the way;

> **He looked at the boy. He could see the disappointment in his face. I'm sorry it's not blue, he said. That's okay, said the boy.**

Some of the readers relate to the idea of having travelled hard and arrived nowhere. Others to staking all their hopes and seeing them dashed. Others still to the idea of having let loved ones down despite their best efforts. We are not despondent, though, because we've spotted the beauty in the lines. It's recognised in the sensitivity of the father, and particularly the son, whose refrain, 'okay', sounds throughout the book as a register of concern for his father, his desire to protect him from the feeling that he's failed his son. Recognising the goodness of characters in a book, even if we've never experienced the like, acts as a little spontaneous revelation of the good guy in us.

As the father and son sit together on the shore, need makes hope:

> **What's on the other side?**
> **Nothing.**
> **There must be something.**
> **Maybe there's a father and his little boy and they're sitting on the beach.**

Mirrors are held up as we read at Phoenix House, too. In the final three sessions of *The Road*, we have a new group member. New inductions to the house are always encouraged to try the reading sessions, and often they return, though many begin with a little skepticism. 'S' seemed to be one of the latter. The first session, he was dismissive and quickly left. The second week he returned but seemed at first only to want to sabotage the session. He didn't like the author, he didn't like the way I was reading. The father and son weren't talking the way he would with his child. He mellowed a little by the close. But the third week he was visibly, actively, in the discussion, and eager to read. He happened to be reading the devastating end of the novel, where the father, dying, tries to comfort his son, to steel him for the continuation of his journey alone:

> **'You have my whole heart. You always did. You're the best guy. You always were. If I'm not here you can still talk to me. You can talk to me and I'll talk to you. You'll see.'**

'S' has to stop reading, hands over to someone else, because he's beginning to feel overcome by the story, by the words – they've made him think of his relationship with his son. I'd had that reaction the first time I read this passage, shedding a tear on the train at Bootle station. There are sounds of consolation in the room, and some defusing laughter. Reading produces long-term, quantifiable changes, but, as any facilitator will know, often the effects are most movingly felt in these moments. You have to be there. What happened when 'S' was reading, his reaction, and our reaction to him, was powerful. It was momentary but we are built on the sustenance of such moments. It was a collective affirmation of what it is to be human. There is no front, no contrivance, no hiding, and because literature provides a distancing buffer, there's no feeling of being exposed, yet 'S', disarmed by the power of words, had shown us the good guy.

YOUR REGULARS

THE LONDON EYE
MY FIRST BOOK

Not long ago, I bought my first book. Now, why should I be so pleased with myself for making such a minor purchase? Surely I should have found my way into an obliging bookstore before now? What I mean is, I acquired a book to publish from the author and his agent, and I will be responsible for it; for editing it, deciding on a cover, convincing colleagues in sales, marketing and publicity of its potential, and finally sending it out into the world, into bookshops, hopefully into bookshop promotions, and ready for purchase.

Buying your first book is part of reaching for the next rung on the career ladder. It is also a little like a gambler's marker (forgive me this, I've been watching *Guys & Dolls*) – it's a pledge, a way of announcing you're in the game. It tells agents and other publishers that your company have confidence enough to put some spending money behind you, and it also tells them what kind of book you're interested in publishing. It feels a lot like slow-motion gambling,

An agent sends round a new manuscript, and you read it, and unlike the last fifty you've read, you like it. With any luck, you think it's the best thing you've read in X number of years in the job, it's ambitious and full of curiosity and insight and real things to say. Once you've decided you're interested in publishing the book, you do some sums based on projected sales figures and work out how much money you could offer the author and agent as an advance on royalties, whilst still making a certain percentage profit. The sales figures are supplied by an experienced colleague in the sales department, which is only fair since they will be the ones trying to convince the bookshops to flog the book if your acquisition is successful. I'll leave aside instances of acquiring books by an author you've already published – that's a whole new book of rules. Let's say you're offering for a highly literary collection of short stories by a first-time author: the colleague in sales will probably give you tiny figures (hopefully over one thousand copies, but perhaps not). This is because the only shops that will definitely sell this unknown highly literary author of short stories are independent bookstores, and maybe Waterstone's. Even if it's a literary novel, no matter how accomplished, the numbers might not be much bigger. You can harangue your colleague in the sales department all you like, you can explain that the unknown young author has a promising future and must be supported, because he/she will probably go on to write a Booker prize-winning novel – but this is the state of the trade. These books are called 'small' (just like Small from *The House at Pooh Corner* – easy to lose or overlook). However, if you're offering for a book with some kind of commercial value, whether because the plot, the author, or a combination of both have a few clear selling points, then the colleague in sales will give you much bigger figures. This is because he or she will definitely be able to sell the book in Waterstone's, get Amazon to price-promote it, probably get it into WH Smiths, and maybe even into the supermarkets.

So you've got your advance, you write/call and tell the agent, putting your best foot forwards. At this point you'll find out how many other publishers are offering on the same book (but not who they are) and whether you've made the highest offer. There can be plenty of surprises at this point. If we're talking about the 'small' literary novel, you've made a small offer (perhaps £5,000) because it should be published but probably won't find a huge audience and this is undeniable fact. But, the agent says they've had an offer from another publisher of £20,000! This other publisher is a regular Skye Masterson, making crazy bids when the odds are clearly stacked against him – there's no way the book will ever earn that much money, no way the advance will ever be paid back in sales. But, in truth, the higher offer is a just reward for the young and talented author, so who cares if the sums don't work?

If we're talking about the more commercial book, it's likely there'll be several offers on the table. Perhaps there's quite a buzz, perhaps it's an American author and the literary scouts have been talking about the manuscript for weeks. (Scouts are some of the most hardworking people in the business; they will read many of the manuscripts on offer or just sold, and provide early reports on their quality and potential to publishers. A trusted scout is a tipster, like a tickbird on a rhinoceros, a valuable asset.) The more publishers involved in an auction, the higher the money will go, forcing anyone who isn't a true high-roller to fold early on. Once the remaining bidders are exhausted, the agent will call best-bids. This is the bit in the gambling game when everyone takes off their watches and rings and throws their car keys on the table; or in the publishing world, you make your highest offer (perhaps only raising your last by a thousand), and write elaborate publishing plans. At some point in the process, if possible, you will try to meet the author and get your colleague from sales, as well as others from marketing and publicity, to meet him or her too. Obviously if the author isn't based in the UK, your publishing plan, usually accompanied by a love-letter to the author, is the main chance to show them that you best understand their work and how to bring it to the reading public.

This whole process usually takes place over about a week, but sometimes longer. The more frantic the bidding process the quicker it's over – this can mean we only have a few days or hours to think about spending a lot of money. But when the process is based on instinct, guess-work, gossip and passion, it probably couldn't be protracted any longer. Finally, when you've put in your final offer, the agent rings you with the answer. 'I'm sorry, but the author felt...' – the reason you lose out is often because you were the underbidder; it's hard for most authors to turn down the offer of more money. But other factors can contribute to winning or losing a book, such as the kind of books you already publish, how well you got on with the author, how convinced they were by your vision for the book.

Hopefully the agent says, 'Congratulations! I'm pleased to say we're going with you'. This is fantastic news, the best you can hear, especially when you've thought about little else for the last few days and suspended your daily work routine and harassed your colleagues to breaking point. But it's elation accompanied by a healthy amount of fear. Because now you've laid down your marker, and the real test is going to be putting all your fine words into practice, and publishing the damn book.

THE READING REVOLUTION

THE ETHOS
FINDING LIFE WORTH LIVING

Jane Davis

Touchstones

At our staff 'think day' a few months ago we talked about The Reader's ethos, and whether we needed to write it down. I have resisted writing anything like an ethos for nearly ten years because as it says at the beginning of Thomas Hardy's novel *Jude the Obscure*, 'the letter killeth'. Of course, deadening happens all the time, in every sphere, in every endeavour, and to almost every person. This is the second law of thermodynamics: systems run down, ideas lose power, stuff goes wrong. 'Things fall off', as Gloucester says in *King Lear*. Especially when the letter cometh in the form of bullet points. The spirit wants better. And that is why literature exists, as one of the world's great poets tells us:

> **Yet the books will be there on the shelves, well born,**
> **Derived from people, but also from radiance, heights.**

Czesław Miłosz's important distinction, that people and books are not the same, is worth remembering. I often want to claim they are pretty much alike and certainly that both books and people should be treated at first meeting with the same open-minded courtesy. Miłosz takes it further and makes books *more than* human. Yes, they come from us, but they also come from 'radiance, heights' and thus, touched by their transcendence, we get beyond ourselves when reading.

With books, when books are working well, we get beyond ourselves but still we remain ourselves, perhaps more presently – here, now – ourselves than at any other time. If this experience was made of electronic components there would be a six-month waiting list. But it's not, it is made of words (and it doesn't matter to me whether those words come on paper or in an ebook). That's why we need the Reading Revolution: we've got to remember what books are, what reading can *do*.

There are many such touchstones; for example, this from William Wordsworth:

Feelings, too,
Of unremembered pleasure: such, perhaps,
As have no slight or trivial influence
On that best portion of a good man's life,
His little, nameless, unremembered, acts
Of kindness and of love.

Wordsworth's idea that good or lovely things pass into us and stay there, affecting us, to be acted out as tiny acts 'of kindness and of love', so ordinary as to be both 'nameless' and 'unremembered' is an invisible building block in our organisation. That is why the first requirement of a Get Into Reading facilitator may be simple kindness, a much under-valued word, which ought to point to empathy: *kind* comes from the Old English word *cynn* – family. Don't mistake it for anything syrupy (though I've nothing against syrup, in the right place). Kindness might some-times be tough, sometimes demanding. It might be about connecting the possibilities beneath the surface, and calling them up. The kindness extends to the books, and they, 'radiant', extend it to us readers. We look for connections, likenesses, points of convergence. So:

- books
- people
- relationship

Will that do? Not really. We need a bit more than that. I was reluctant but thought it might be good to remember the beginning – perhaps I would *feel* the ethos there?

Beginning

The Reader Organisation began life as *The Reader* magazine, in Spring 1997. Before that, it existed, but not in its own right, in practice in the Departments of Continuing Education and of English at the University of Liverpool. The first time we used the name *The Reader* was when we put together the first issue of this magazine. Other contenders for the title were 'The Abercromby Pig', and 'The Mersey'. I don't remember how we arrived at *The Reader* (I was in favour of the pig). That first issue had a mildly self-effacing attitude marked by not putting the editorial at the front and not even calling it an editorial. There's something wrong with that, but the impulse – we're all in this together – was right. In that unacknowledged editorial we wrote:

Literature, we believe, exists to address the hunger for truth. Readers read to assuage needs that exist (as Wordsworth has it) 'too deep for tears'.

In retrospect it is clear that we had the nub of the matter right there at the beginning, when the first issue quoted from Saul Bellow's novel, *Herzog*. The hero is talking about his teaching in classes very like our own in the Continuing Education programme. Students in evening classes don't come for 'culture', Herzog says, they come for reality:

people are dying – it is no metaphor – for lack of something real to carry home when day is done

Our courses were practical: based on building shared understandings through slow shared reading – and we read aloud, not whole books, as we do now in Get Into Reading, but lots of important chunks, so that the text had a presence in the room.

Many people who came to those classes had university educations and professional lives. And like any group of human beings they also had problems: illnesses both physical and mental, sometimes life-threatening, severe, enduring; loneliness, loss of powers, loss of loves, unhappy marriages, problems with children or parents, jobs that were too pressured, no job at all, loss of purpose, the presence of death.

Looking back, it is easy to see that those literature classes offered some sort of practical value to all of us – teachers and students – during hard personal times. This was not so easy to see at the time. These were 'courses', taking place in a university. There is a formality to such proceedings, an impersonality. But for me that impersonality dissolved as pressures in my personal life forced the reality of the literature into me. I will give one example, though I might supply a dozen. At one point a family member was in enormous distress: there was no fix, and it seemed that whatever happened, someone would suffer. I remember teaching a session on George Herbert's poem 'Affliction IV' in which this terrifying poem taught me something about the situation in which I found myself.

> **BROKEN in pieces all asunder,**
>   **Lord, hunt me not,**
>   **A thing forgot,**
> **Once a poor creature, now a wonder,**
>   **A wonder tortured in the space**
>   **Betwixt this world and that of grace.**
>
> **My thoughts are all a case of knives,**
>   **Wounding my heart**
>   **With scattered smart ;**

As wat'ring-pots give flowers their lives.
  Nothing their fury can control,
  While they do wound and prick my soul.

All my attendants are at strife
    Quitting their place
    Unto my face :
Nothing performs the task of life :
  The elements are let loose to fight,
  And while I live, try out their right.

Oh help, my God ! let not their plot
    Kill them and me,
    And also Thee,
Who art my life : dissolve the knot,
  As the sun scatters by his light
  All the rebellions of the night.

Then shall those powers which work for grief,
    Enter Thy pay,
    And day by day
Labour Thy praise and my relief :
  With care and courage building me,
  Till I reach heav'n, and much more, Thee.

When I brought this to class there is no doubt my students could sense a reality in my reading, and what's more I felt compelled to make that reality visible by asking students to 'translate' the poem into possible contemporary, recognisable scenarios.

Someone said, when you are 'broken in pieces all asunder' the last thing you want is someone searching you out, looking for you, because you don't want to be seen, you don't want to be found in this broken state. This might be, ventured another class member, the state of someone seeing a psychiatrist for the first time. An addict entering rehab and not wanting to be cured, said someone else. A pupil, with problems, avoiding the very teacher who might help them sort themselves out. Not going to the doctor when you are depressed. Not eating.

We spoke about how that carefully arranged line, 'Nothing performs the task of life' perfectly holds the incapacity of depression, dis-ease, trauma. 'Nothing', starting the line, seemed a powerful presence, almost a being in its own right. That life is a 'task' rather than something that simply, naturally happens, seemed symptomatic of the difficulty of living in, through, or with, intense inner problems.

And we read the poem as if it was real. It was real – offering a language, a structure, in which to think otherwise unbearable and chaotic thoughts. 'Derived from people, but also from radiance, heights'.

A few guidelines

As I worked on 'the ethos' – asking colleagues to read what I had written, to help and to comment – I began to realise that the part of me that was reluctant to write it down was not so much afraid that 'the letter killeth' as that you can't, unless you are a much better writer than I am, get much into a small space. I need now to write a book about The Reader Organisation, The Reading Revolution, Get Into Reading. But in the meantime the organisation is using these temporary, stop-gap, but will-do-for-now guidelines. Happy to hear from you if you've got improvements, suggestions or complexities that can go into the book.

Reading Literature
We see reading as a way of feeling and thinking about being alive, and start from the assumption that great literature is the most *inclusive* and *useful* art-form, that even difficult or ancient works can be made accessible. We call 'great literature' any piece of writing that gives what Bernard Malamud in his novel *The Assistant* called 'the crazy sensation you are reading about yourself'. And if not yourself then something or someone you recognise, or want to know. It is not a fixed canon, and depends on who 'you' are. We want to read across the centuries and across cultures – because great writers have lived in all places, in all ages – and would be just as likely to try to read *The Epic of Gilgamesh* or *The Winter's Tale* as *The Wasp Factory* or *The World's Wife*.

Reading Aloud
Reading aloud is not simply a way of getting around literacy problems: it is an experience in its own right, which generates particular and unique responses in individuals and groups. For us, the act of slow reading involves a deeply personal response, but we read as accurately as possible, testing what is read with what's inside ourselves. Do I know that? Can I imagine that? Is there any way of translating these stranger-words into something I can understand?

Why Do We Do It?
Some effects of Get Into Reading are: to grow or strengthen individuals' love of reading, to build kindness and community between people, and to open up the great books to those who would not otherwise read them. The Reader Organisation believes that people write great books in order to pass on wisdom, and we read them to get it. The getting of wisdom is sometimes a painful, sometimes a pleasurable process. The sharing can alleviate the pain a little, and certainly magnifies the pleasure.

YOUR REGULARS

ASK THE READER

Brian Nellist

Q Looking at my back numbers of *The Reader* am I wrong in sniffing out a certain bias, mainly lying in the assumptions made by many of the writers, towards a preference for 'realism', especially maybe the Victorian realist novel? Because, if so, I have qualms. If the question of what is 'real' could be settled so definitely, why then does the inventiveness and fantasy of romance and science fiction continue to find so large a readership? I hesitate to use a term like 'transcendence' but surely that is what realism by implication denies?

A You are probably right but there is a danger, I think, in giving a spurious clarity to that term 'realist'. The novel is traditionally thought to come into being by setting itself more rigid limits for the probable than earlier prose narratives. There are in Defoe and Richardson no miracles or magic or kings and queens such as we find in romances like Sidney's *Arcadia*. They remain in a recognisable world which is why Walter Scott thought that the novel was always historical – it showed human manners and beliefs at a distinct moment in time. But both these founding fathers of the novel still invoke a Being and values that transcend the material explanations of life, which indeed causes confusions about how to act in the minds of the protagonists and certainly for the other characters, as with Crusoe, Friday or Moll Flanders and for Squire B. and Lovelace in Richardson. If Victorian novels are often less theologically explicit that does not mean that truth-seeking characters in them do not question the self-contentment of the average sensual men or women they encounter. Immanence does not wholly replace transcendence, to use your term, when in *Middlemarch* Dorothea Brooke tells Ladislaw that 'by discovering what is perfectly good, even when we don't quite know what it is and cannot do what we would, we are part of the divine power against evil'. The qualification, within a qualification, 'even when we don't *quite* know what it is' transforms what might simply be a rational moralism into a tentative belief. In that Dorothea and George Eliot are representative in going beyond the limits of the everyday. The challenge to material satisfaction often comes from negative sources. It is not morbidity but as a rebuke to self-sufficiency that the incidents of mortality occur so frequently in the novels of Dickens and Mrs Gaskell, for example. Little Paul Dombey on whom such great expectations depend hears the waves whispering the dreaded word death and asks his outraged father what is the use of money when it could not save his mother from death. The fact of our mortality is what permanently transcends our existence. 'What shall it profit a man, if he shall gain the whole world, and lose his own soul' is what Dombey should have recalled, as Dickens undoubtedly did.

Twentieth century critics coined the term 'Magic Realism' as though it were a specific form but in a way realism always reinvents magic as it seeks to explore the limits of its own apparent assumptions. It tells a story and stories depend upon coincidence, repetitions, doublings and situations which reverberate in the collective human memory. There is a kind of providence at work which makes the end always present in the beginning and whether that is benign or destructive marks not only the difference between comedy and tragedy but also that relation to 'transcendence' which the author holds to be the 'real'. Is *Jane Eyre* a realist novel? Certainly in terms of the detail with which identities and situations are presented the restrictions of realism are being observed. Though the madwoman in the attic may devolve from the terrors of Otranto and Udolpho, she is there to remind the reader that though Jane herself is extreme in her passions and often filled with comparable rage she can contain her actions by obedience to other values. Her realism fights to transcend the inner dangers but it is supported by a kind of magic. If the lightning that strikes the ancient chestnut before the intended bigamous marriage is a warning from beyond then it is balanced by a voice calling 'Jane, Jane, Jane', that saves her from a merely dutiful marriage to the ascetic St John Rivers, good man though he is. That might seem an unfair instance to adduce from the very edge of realism but it is no more stretched than, for example, the arrest of

Tess at Stonehenge after she and Angel Clare have at last consummated their love in Hardy's novel. The extreme use of coincidence and symbol in his work is not a wanton manipulation of plot but an expression of his belief that the conditions of life are inimical to the values that human beings most respect, tolerance, tenderness, constancy and love. All that talk of the President of the Immortals is only a metaphor for his belief that we long for transcendence yet that which commands the individual life actually opposes it. What is beyond is really beneath us, what is above is really below us.

The world of earlier twentieth-century novelists, reconstructing the model of the perceived world from the inside out might seem to accommodate the visionary and the transcendental more readily, though Lawrence and Virginia Woolf both admired George Eliot and their work evolves out of hers. That reflecting voice in the Victorian novel commenting on the action of the book which, after James the later writers eschewed, is in its way a radical fracturing of the realist surface. 'Trust the tale and not the teller' Lawrence urges us, but rather listen to both and allow the greater sense of reality's mysteriousness to grow in your mind. It is that gap between event, person, situation and mind which both centuries' realists are writing in. If that seems too cosy a judgement then it is our own perceptions as readers which shift, often in the same person, between sometimes seeing the difference and at others the continuity. 'Even when we don't quite know what it is' seems a valid guide to most forms of judgement in this area.

YOUR REGULARS

OUR SPY IN NY
CAN YOU BE READING THAT?

Enid Stubin

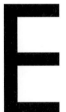ven the irreligious keep their days of observance, and your spy is no exception, having topped off a day of fasting and sulking with a smoked fish extravaganza at my brother's new apartment. At the table I caught scraps of conversation over horrible books that people read for their clubs and loved, like the maddeningly titled *The Reader*, by Bernhard Schlink. Not so much designated as simply having assumed the role of family curmudgeon, I knew I had to tread softly. My nephew, a darling fellow, asked me what I thought of Jonathan Franzen: Was he really the great contemporary American novelist? Only if one had given up on the contemporary American novel, and in some ways I had. Eric's wife, a wry and spirited young woman, adored *Let the Great World Spin* and was impressed to learn that I knew Colum McCann. I have to say, I'm impressed myself. Suzy enjoys the idea of the New York novel but draws the line at anything written before 1995. Can I convince her, do you think, to take up *The House of Mirth*?

The other day I went to a poetry reading: a small publishing house was throwing a launch for a new title, Hardy's 'Poems of 1912–13' and other poems about Emma. The book, called *Unexpected Elegies*, is a doty thing, beautifully produced in paperback and suitable for gift-giving, as the marketers announce round about October. When I got to the venue, a posh bookstore on the Upper East Side, the place was so filled with Republicans that the polite silence took one aback. The women were immaculately coiffed, sporting serious designer togs – I'm talking Carolina Herrera and Valentino. The men were all in suits and ties and tortoiseshell glasses. When the waters parted I did see a few reliably literary types, male and female, in tank tops and jeans.

I make it a point to buy whatever's being sold at a reading, but I drew the line at two full-length volumes by a New York figurehead whose ordinary verse carries heavy-duty cachet. Despite looking like a low-level gangster in a fifties B-movie, he's the head of an important non-profit organization and is perceived to dole out whacking gobs of grant money for scholarship and the arts. I'd heard of him but had never seen him, and listening to him read Hardy's poems of mourning depressed me, quite possibly for all the wrong reasons. The crowd, clucking and nodding, warmed to the middleweight ironies of their composition: completely indifferent to Emma for most of their married life, Hardy fashioned himself into the adoring, grief-knackered husband only after her death. And the poet's reading struck them as the real thing. You rarely see the business of literature conducted so blatantly.

After the sonorities I waited in line to have my copy signed by an elegant Brahmin whose editorial help was lauded as 'invaluable' by the publishers. When I told her my name, she remembered me as having helped *her* editorially – a long poem she'd contributed to an anthology of verse about music had caught on a thorn about halfway through stanza two, and I must have posed some cogent suggestions. I must have posed them tactfully, because she scrawled a gracious envoi with a flourish, her Schlumberger rings glinting in the light. She'd certainly filled the place with her Episcopalian peeps, and as I made way for them to greet her, I caught the attention of a woman who was yammering about books not her own and asking me if I recognized the poets in the room, some of whom looked far too good for credibility in form-fitting black T-shirts, a late-summer uniform of sorts. Fearful that she'd make introductions, I looked around for access to the table where Shiraz was being poured carefully if not lavishly, swallowed some and nodded. My interlocutor complained that her teenage son had been forced to read *The Assistant* over the summer. That's one of the great novels written in English, I said, too quietly. Was I *sure*? *The Assistant*? About a grocery? So *grim*, she moaned. But she *had* enjoyed *Life of Pi*. I chewed my way through a fifth handful of sugar-toasted peanuts and wondered what to do with my face.

This past week someone reminded me that having seen him with a copy of *The Girl with the Dragon Tattoo*, I'd asked contemptuously, 'You're reading *that*?' I couldn't remember this incident and questioned whether I'd bother to have revealed my distaste for a book read by more people worldwide than *Uncle Tom's Cabin*. That doesn't sound like me to me. Recovering from surgery, my cousin Shirley had sent her brother Lester and me on a vital errand to procure a reserved copy of *The Girl* from her local public library branch, and she pounced on it when we delivered the goods. Why would I object to its reception? No, no, he insisted, I'd been absolutely scathing, and he'd felt 'put down'. Too weary to defend the cause of literature, if not myself, I made a note never to respond to anything anyone was reading. Ever. It's more personal than you can imagine.

At The Store I've already offended colleagues over the latest title for Kingsborough Reads, *The Glass Castle*. Having fought the choice last January in a series of blistering e-mails that happily went ignored, I'm now teaching the book in my developmental (read: remedial) class, where my students chafe under its author's winsome denial and psychological evasions. I'm plotting to get *Let the Great World Spin* accepted for next year. An administrator at the table allowed as to how she'd been *this close* to signing Toni Morrison for an author's event, and wouldn't it be wonderful if we could read *The Bluest Eye* next year? *This close* to Toni Morrison didn't deliver her to our shores – we'd be as likely to sign Marie of Romania – and my resistance to the novel didn't need venting.

On an expedition last week to a glossy Manhattan bookstore, I did my best to distract my nephew's little daughter, a hungry reader who was spending a long weekend with her Nana and Papa and missing her mommy something fierce. Ambling along the aisles of paperbacks, I tugged out this title and that, hoping to console a listless Alex. But she owned this one, and that one didn't pass muster, and I concentrated on replacing some Spiderman facetiousness for her younger brother Matthew. Then I remembered the series I'd loved at eight. Sydney Taylor's *All-of-a-Kind Family* books chronicled the lives of working-class immigrants on the Lower East Side and opened with that most awful of domestic calamities – a lost library book. And there, amid the schlocky Young Adult romances and the redoubtable *Captain Underpants* oeuvre, was a lone copy. Triumphant, I snatched it up and handed it to Alex, but not even the promise of dessert at the café could lure her out of homesickness. Over coffee and Rice Krispies treats I took care not to push my find but bought the book anyway and tucked it away for the return home: a New York novel for two – maybe three – generations of big-city readers.

THE READER CROSSWORD

Cassandra   No.32

ACROSS

1. Administrative body initially providing quite useful and necessary growth overseas (6)
4. Sounds like a visionary view of the basis of capitalist economics (6)
* 9 and 26 across. Our heroine's name changed to Barryman (4, 6)
10. Chiastic manuscript developed a tendency to split (10)
11. Hairstyle popular in Edinburgh (6)
* 12 and 23 down. Like chalk and cheese, poles apart (5, 3, 5)
13. Alps encircle the spot where the man from North Wales makes his home (4,5)
15. Prison courtyard? (4)
16. Role reversal trick (4)
* 17 and 3 down. She was named for a queen but published as a wife (9, 7)
* 21. Cheshire town occupied by Amazons (8)
22. Intricate South African lace produced in this wine region (6)
24. What lorry did to lay-by possibly led to lupin display (6, 4)
25. State in which nothing but a head can be seen (4)
* 26. See 9 across
27. Is a life force disturbed on this volcanic island? (6)

DOWN

1. Missile a reason for disagreement (7)
2. Indo-European language speakers in family background of Mary and Anne (5)
*3. See 17 across
5. To go to Nice for example (6)
6. Startling evidence of paparazzi presence (9)
7. Like Viola and Sebastian, or most towns today (7)
8. Angel dust for keeping horses quiet (13)
14. Confused student foreigner could be killer (9)
16. Inside this super turbine is the power to make one anxious (7)
18. These fanatics stole a last letter mistakenly (7)
19. Baroque composition produced by two cats and a duck fighting (7)
20. This cult has its beginnings in very odd ornamentation discovered on obelisk (6)
* 23. See 12 across

*Clues with an asterisk have a common theme

OXFORD
UNIVERSITY PRESS

BUCK'S QUIZ

ALL SINGING, ALL DANCING

Angela Macmillan

1. Which way is Violet Hetherington dancing on a transatlantic cruise ship to New York?

2. Where do the five Mundy sisters do their dancing?

3. Pauline, Petrova and Posy are orphaned babies adopted by the eccentric fossil collector and explorer Gum. What do they go on to wear, according to the title of this book?

4. In which long poem will you find, 'On with the dance! Let joy be unconfined'?

5. Who observed: 'Swans sing before they die – 'twere no bad thing / Did certain persons die before they sing'?

6. *Swan Song* concludes the second trilogy in which novel sequence?

7. *Places Where They Sing* is the sixth novel in which sequence?

8. Who sang with Berenice and John Henry 'in the August kitchen after it was dark'?

9. Whose dancing was 'awkward and solemn, apologising instead of attending, and often moving wrong without being aware of it,' bringing 'shame and misery' to his partner?

10. In which short story does Leila have a 'Darling little pink – and – silver [dance] programme with pink pencils and fluffy tassels'?

11. 'My heart was shaken with tears; and horror / Drifted away'. What caused this?

12. 'When I am dead my dearest'. What shouldn't 'my dearest' do then?

13. What is the profession of Prince Turveydrop?

14. What is the name of the artist's model and laundress who is transformed into a great diva in Paris.

15. 'Will you, won't you, will you, won't you, won't you join the dance?' What is the name of the dance?

PRIZES!

The winner of the Crossword (plucked in time-honoured tradition from a hat) will receive our selection of World's Classics paperbacks, and the same to the winner of the fiendishly difficult Buck's Quiz.

Congratulations to Tony Anstey, Birkenhead (Crossword) and to Heather Jones, Newcastle, Staffs (winner Buck's Quiz).

Please send your solutions (marked either Cassandra Crossword, or Buck's Quiz) to 19 Abercromby Square, Liverpool L69 7ZG.

ANSWERS

CASSANDRA CROSSWORD NO. 31

Across
1. Staring 5. Electro 9. Metro 10. And George 11. Cautionary 12. Land 14. Calceolarias 18. Intolerantly 21. Soho 22. Coloratura 25. In Siberia 26. Cairn 27. Kingdom 28. Assents

Down
1. Sumach 2. Arthur 3. Ironically 4. Grain 5. Eiderdown 6. Eden 7. Terrapin 8. Overdose 13. Dalliances 15. Cartogram 16. Dipstick 17. At the Sun 19. Julian 20. Barnes 23. Obama 24. Abed

BUCK'S QUIZ NO. 39

1. *The Princess*, Tennyson 2. *The African Queen* 3. *Richard II* 4. *Restoration*, Rose Tremain 5. *The Snow Queen* 6. To become kings 7. *The Faerie Queene* 8. Queen Elizabeth II 9. *The Happy Prince*, Oscar Wilde 10. Prince Andrei Bolkonsky, *War and Peace* 11. Queen Mab 12. *Huntingtower*, John Buchan 13. King Arthur 14. Machiavelli in *The Prince* 15. The Red Queen, *Through the Looking Glass*

FICTION

THE HOLLOW MEN WITHOUT MASKS

Rob Magnuson Smith

I let the younger lawyers lay waste to the oysters and Grey Goose martinis. I rode the escalator alone, up toward the glass roof of the Seattle Art Museum.

My firm had rented out the museum to celebrate a sizable class action victory, and nobody had left the reception area all night. Here we were, surrounded by art, and everyone stood clumped together in suits, slurping and gobbling and carrying on. For fifteen months we'd been working seven days a week. This was supposed to be our celebration. I couldn't unwind. I'd had a martini that only made me sober. Then, while leaning over a platter of smoked halibut, I'd been struck by a strange tightening of my throat, as if victimized by a bored God harassing people nearing forty. These recent law school grads didn't understand – before they knew it, they'd look like me.

Riding the escalator cheered me up. As I rose toward the stars on my little traveling step, the museum opened in all directions. I passed an installment of *papier-mâché* Model-T Fords dangling from the ceiling. I moved through centuries of paintings, sculptures, and artifacts. The sound of grazing lawyers faded beneath me, and I had the pleasant sensation of leaving them permanently on the ground floor of the museum, where they'd be mummified, catalogued, and placed on display.

At the top floor I stepped off the escalator. I started walking and set in motion the automatic ceiling lights. A docent in a green jacket appeared against a wall. He'd been standing in the dark beside a glass case of African tribal masks, perhaps doing his best to stay awake. As I came toward him, and the lights continued to cascade across the ceiling, he straightened up and brushed his hair with his fingers.

I studied my museum map and waited for the docent to pull himself together. He was stooped and elderly, about the age of my father. Then I remembered my father had died a few months back – maybe it had been a year. He'd been a lawyer, too. I tried to visit him in the hospital after his heart attack, but he hadn't let me stay longer than a couple of minutes. 'Go back to the office,' he'd insisted, waving his wrinkly hand. 'Don't waste billable hours on a corpse.'

I'd landed in the Africa wing. The map said my favorite European paintings were located on the floor below. But as the empty down escalator squeaked toward the lower floors, I realized I had the run of the place. Why not start with Africa? The docent nodded as I approached his display case, as if approving my decision.

The tribal masks sat on sticks. Even behind glass, they looked frightening – a hyena with an elongated jaw, an ivory serpent head with a ten-foot conical tail, a hairy antelope adorned with bones, dried sinews, and teeth. One wooden mask had square eye holes and no mouth. It was painted, the notecard informed me, with a patina of sacrificial blood. Jesus, I thought, get me down to the Impressionists, with their sun-dappled tea parties and water lilies and bathing French families. I noticed a placard:

For African tribe members, masks provide a socially sanctioned vehicle for transcending the confines of the ego. A mask can help resolve existential problems brought on by the spirit forces that guided the mask's creation. Tribe members are encouraged to gather during ritual dance and view the mask in action, since beneficial results can occur from maintaining an open emotional disposition.

I moved along the display case with my hands in my pockets, wary of awakening any dormant emotions. You might say I've spent my entire life in this fashion. Each time I've tried to date, start a hobby, or even take a vacation, my job has intervened like some divine force – a presence I invited into my home without expecting it to stay for good. But tonight I found myself stopping for what seemed an eternity under the gaze of a smiling chimp. He had a circular wooden face, glass eyes, reddish cheeks. His smile was both friendly and unsettling. He sent images flashing through my mind. Had I once worn this mask, along with a leather thong and a necklace of bones? Could that have been me outside a hut, dancing in front of a fire in an attempt to transcend the confines of my ego?

'These are all aimed at ancestor worship.'

The docent stood beside me, cleaning his teeth with his pinky. There was cigarette ash on the lapels of his jacket, and he smelled like a tuna sandwich. 'When the young'ens get uppity, the older guys put on these masks to scare'em.'

'But it says here,' I said, 'that these masks resolve existential problems.'

'No longer the working theory,' the docent said, raising himself on his toes. 'They brought in an expert, and I attended her lecture on the matter. We gotta update the placard.'

'Sure,' I said, indulging him. I had convinced myself that I'd become something of an expert myself. 'So it's all about ancestors, is it?'

'Ancestor worship.'

The docent pulled a ring of keys from his belt and opened the glass case. 'See, after you die, your soul comes back – maybe in the form of an ox, or maybe something like this.' The docent brought out the hyena with jagged teeth and placed it over his head. His voice carried through the elongated mouth and echoed off the walls. 'The kids would get a reminding that the old folks could return any time to set 'em straight.'

I took a step toward the escalator. I was alone with a man wearing a hyena head. 'You been working here long?'

'Since the exhibit opened in '81. Each day of work is a blessing, I think. You with that gang down there?'

I felt my ears redden. Each day of work is a blessing – it was something my dad used to say. 'We lawyers,' I said, 'are not exactly the most adventurous group. I doubt you'll see anybody else up here tonight.'

'Fine by me,' the docent said. He coughed dust out of the hyena mouth. 'I like to have plenty of time to poke around.'

'I can see that.' I glanced at my chimp. The docent noticed.

'You want to try that puppy on?'

'I don't think that's wise.'

He took it out of the case. 'Balsam, chimp hair, blood, and glass for the eyeballs. Ivory Coast,' he added, fitting the mask against my face and tying the string in back.

I looked at the docent through the glass chimp eyes. His hyena head shimmered like something on the other end of a kaleidoscope. Maybe I imagined it, but I smelled traces of a campfire.

'Say something through the mouth,' the docent suggested.

'Do they use human blood to paint these masks?'

'Put some emotion into it. Don't worry, we're alone up here.'

'Each day of work is a blessing.'

The docent shook his leather hyena ears. 'You really believe that?'

'What do you think?' I kicked at the floor. 'I've got thirty years before I can even think of retiring. These new guys – they need to be warned.'

We faced each other in our respective masks and sustained an uncomfortable silence. 'I need to get back to the reception,' I said.

The docent untied the string behind my head. He took my chimp away and tucked it under his arm. My face felt suddenly naked. I rubbed my jaw and waited for it to return – the stiffening of my lips, the familiar squint around my eyes.

'Why don't you wear your mask down there?' The docent chuckled through his hyena teeth. 'Shake things up a bit.'

I cinched up my tie. I started to leave and stopped when I saw that he meant it.

'You gotta wear it,' he said, pointing at the placard, 'while your tribe is gathered.'

'You said that was no longer the working theory.'

'Maybe it's never been tested, anthropologically speaking. Don't the real experts do that?'

'Not with my life they don't.' I wasn't sure I wanted to relinquish my ego. What would be left behind?

'Arrgh,' the docent said, lowering his hyena head. He clapped his hands and threw out his elbows. 'Howl and arrgh!'

I watched him dance. He came toward me once more with my chimp, and I didn't feel capable of resisting. 'You'll have to bring it back, of course,' he said, placing the mask back on my face and tying it up. 'Give me a report on how it went.'

The docent guided me to the escalator and sent me down to the lower floors. Through the mask, the museum looked like a playground. I passed the paintings and sculptures and *papier-mâché* Model-T Fords – works of so many children. I breathed the smoke of African campfires and grinned under the mask to release my inner chimp.

There was laughter and conversation, ice rattling in cocktail shakers. My colleague Bernie slouched over the cheese. Then someone pointed. I lifted my hands in the air as everyone fell silent, and I let the lights of the reception burn into my glass eyes. It was the first time I ever felt in control without knowing what would happen next.

CONTRIBUTORS

Linda Chase lives in Manchester. She's director of *Poets & Players*, a poetry and music series. She's currently working on a new book to be published by Carcanet in October 2011. Her previous titles are *The Wedding Spy* and *Extended Family.*

Terence Davies, film director was born in Liverpool in 1945. His films include *Distant Voices, Still Lives* (1988), *The Long Day Closes* (1992), *The House of Mirth* (2000) and most recently, his first documentary, *Of Time and the City* (2008).

Tessa Hadley lives in Cardiff and teaches at Bath Spa University. She has published three novels and one collection of stories; her new novel, *The London Train*, comes out in January 2011.

Rob Magnuson Smith's debut novel *The Gravedigger* recently won the William Faulkner Award and is published by University of New Orleans Press. Raised in England and the state of Oregon, he is currently the Doctoral Research Fellow in Creative Writing at Bath Spa University.

Emma McGordon was named as one of the 'top ten literary stars' of 2008 by *The Times* online; she is also a former winner of the Northern Young Writer of the Year Award. Her book *Those Who Jump* is available from www.tall-lighthouse.co.uk.

Ian McMillan was born in 1956 and has been a freelance writer/performer /broadcaster since 1981. He presents *The Verb* on BBC Radio 3 every Friday night.

Alexis McNay is a project worker with Get Into Reading.

Richard Meier lives in London with his wife and baby daughter, and works in mental health policy. His pamphlet is due to be published by Happenstance in 2011 and he has been shortlisted for the Picador Poetry Prize 2010.

Matt Merritt is a poet and wildlife journalist from Leicester. His collection, *hydrodaktulopsychicharmonica*, is out now from Nine Arches Press, following *Troy Town* (2008) and *Making The Most Of The Light* (2005). He blogs at http://polyolbion.blogspot.com/

Blake Morrison is a poet and author. His memoir, *And When Did You Last See Your Father?* won the J.R. Ackerly Prize for Autobiography. Non-fiction books include *As If* (1997), about the James Bulger case. His latest novel, *The Last Weekend* was published in May 2010.

Brian Murray teaches at Loyola University Maryland. He is a contributor to the *Continuum Encyclopedia of British Literature* and is the author of the *Bedside, Bathtub & Armchair Companion to Dickens*.

Catherine Pickstock is a Reader in Philosophy and Theology at the University of Cambridge. She has written books and articles in the area of philosophical theology. Her current project is a book about theory, religion and idiom in Platonic philosophy.

Peter Robinson's most recent book of poetry is *English Nettles and Other Poems* (Two Rivers), published in 2010 along with a book of literary criticism, *Poetry & Translation: The Art of the Impossible* (Liverpool), and *An Unofficial Roy Fisher* (Shearsman), His edition of Bernard Spencer's *Complete Poetry, Translations & Selected Prose* (Bloodaxe), a translation of *Poems* by Antonia Pozzi (One World Classics), and *Reading Poetry: An Anthology* (Two Rivers) are forthcoming in 2011.

Michael Schmidt is Professor of Poetry at Glasgow University. He is editorial director of Carcanet Press and general editor of *PN Review.* He is a critic and literary historian. Collected Poems was published by Smith/Doorstop in 2009.

Enid Stubin is Assistant Professor of English at Kingsborough Community College of the City University of New York and Adjunct Professor of Humanities at NY University's School of Continuing and Professional Studies.

Distribution Information

Trade orders Contact Mark Chilver, Magazine Department, Central Books
email: mark@centralbooks.com
web: www.centralbooks.com
tel: 0845 458 9925   fax: 0845 458 9912
Central Books, 99 Wallis Road, London, E9 5LN

For any other queries regarding trade orders or institutional subscriptions, please contact Lee Keating in The Reader Office

email: leekeating@thereader.org.uk   tel: 0151 794 2830